ACKNOWLEDGMENTS

Tamiris, you are my loving and supportive wife, my best friend, companion, and the devoted mother of our wonderful son. Without your continuous support and enduring patience listening to my never ending difficulties, this book could not have been written. Your wonderful ability to make significant suggestions throughout the project gave me the energy needed to make my vision a reality. In doing so, your intellect and philosophy on life were an inspiration. For all those reasons and so much more, this endeavor is dedicated to you and our son.

Simply put, because of Mark C. Yerger this project actually started and was completed. He was continually behind me with an unlimited willingness to help and inspire, particularly when my motivation wavered at the unforeseen difficulties, learning aspects, and unexpected time involved. His magnanimity and patience in assisting me with creating the final result involved literally hundreds of hours, and in return he simply and only wanted me to strive for the most detail and exactness. His imprint on the project can simply not be described in words and I deeply appreciate his tutelage. He made it all possible, and I know Otto is very proud of him.

My personal friend and former "Leibstandarte" staff officer Hans Bernhard was always available when I had questions. My seemingly endless inquiries about the Division, his personal experiences pertaining to Theodor Wisch, or other unit commanders, were always politely replied in detail. Even at 90 years old he was unwavering with his responses to my continual quest for details. His sensitivity and ability to accurately evaluate personalities never ceased to amaze me. I thank him for the countless hours of discussion by phone and mail. His hospitality, the appetizing sandwiches he prepared, and the cherries provided for my family and me during our visit at his home were all wonderfully memorable. Sadly Hans Bernhard passed away on October 2, 2010, before this book was published.

I deeply appreciate my long time friend, John M. Donovan, for supporting me throughout the years. His assistance in locating and helping me acquire many of Wisch's original documents and other "Leibstandarte" material can be seen throughout this volume. I can't express the enjoyment his help has given in owning the pieces of time related to this officer who has so captivated my interest.

My close local friend Jaime Sadurni must be thanked for his role in keeping me on track and motivated to continuously gather photos and documents for a potential Wisch project. If I'd ceased acquiring material years ago when I'd considered doing so, the book would lack many of Wisch's personal documents and photos that are now shown.

My thanks as well as respect to the former members of the "Leibstandarte" and other Waffen-SS units who provided assistance and support. These include Ernst Barkmann (Knight's Cross), Hans-Werner Christians, Erhard Gührs, Waldemar Heinrich, Otto Kumm (Swords holder and last commander of the "Leibstandarte"), Rudolf von Ribbentrop (Knight's Cross), Kurt Sametreiter (Knight's Cross), Franz Schmitz, Heinrich Springer (Knight's Cross), Jupp Steinbüchel, and Harry Wulf.

Private individuals who contributed their time and material were appreciated throughout the project. Bertino Adler, Peter Buchner, Etienne Braspenning, Thomas Fischer, John Koser, Jeffrey Nichols, Patrick Ott, Steve Pardon, Hans-Peter Rackete, Andreas Schulz, Mike Smeets, Charles Trang, and Neill Thomson all added to this hopefully complete study of Theodor Wisch.

Special thanks also to my mother Maren, Hartmut, and my brother Martin for their love and support. My thoughts also go to my father, Johann, who passed away too early in January 2010.

Finally, my respects to Theodor Wisch. My interest in his significant military career expanded to understanding his entire life and the events within it. I hope he would see this work as an accurate and objective examination created simply for the historical purpose of preserving a record of his life and experiences.

FOREWORD

As a young soldier in the Waffen-SS I served with Infantry Regiment "Deutschland," and after attending Junkerschule Braunschweig, as an officer in the "Leibstandarte SS Adolf Hitler" during World War II. I experienced war and all its horrible aspects from the beginning of the 1939 Polish campaign through the capitulation on May 8, 1945, in Austria.

My military career led me from serving with the infantry in Poland, to the artillery regiment of the "Leibstandarte," and finally to its divisional staff. From the summer of 1944 I served as Third General Staff Officer (Ic), then temporarily as First General Staff Officer (Ia), and finally as First Ordnance Officer (O1). In Normandy as temporary divisional Ia, I fought next to Brigadeführer Wisch during the fierce defensive battles against the Allies. There I got to know him as an always dependable comrade and brave leader. When he was severely wounded near Falaise on August 20, 1944, I personally evacuated him from the battlefield.

I am pleased the author has undertaken the task of writing a detailed biography of the second commander of the "Leibstandarte" and hope it is well received by those interested in the history of the Waffen-SS.

Hans Bernhard
Hauptsturmführer a.D.
Ic, O1 and Ia i.V.
1.SS-Panzer-Division "Leibstandarte"

INTRODUCTION

Germany's military history, like other countries at the time, had long traditions and a social class system that determined the success of careers, a vocation attractive to many of the period. Among the newer concepts initiated by the SS-Verfügungstruppe was a system based on ability and ignorant of social origins of soldiers, along with more modern training and tactical methods compared to the Army still based in the previous war, to some extent.

Among the classic units, perhaps the best known and among the most studied is the "Leibstandarte," a formation originally created as Hitler's personal guard unit and in various title changes incorporating his name. While portions of it continued in that role in the wartime period, it expanded to become a front line combat unit and first saw action in the 1939 Polish campaign.

As created in 1933 it was an elite formation, and that status saw it receiving the best available equipment throughout its history. An initial lack of sufficient formal military training was quickly advanced with the input of other SS/VT units and commanders, notably the influx junior officers graduating from the SS officer school system created by Paul Hausser. For much of its history the "Leibstandarte" is synonymous with Sepp Dietrich, its initial commander. The combat successes of the unit are, of course, based on the efforts of its individual soldiers. The leadership skills and resulting devotion accorded its first commander were combined with a staff and element commanders who exceeded or otherwise complimented Dietrich's lack of formal large formation training. He fostered the careers of the men who complimented his command style, creating the officer corps that was so successful. While the eventual "Das Reich," "Totenkopf," "Polizei," and "Wiking" Divisions were formed first, the status of the "Leibstandarte" saw it eventually holding the initial number in the formation titles sequence, even though it did not become a full division until 1941.

The "Leibstandarte" attained legendary status during its existence and produced some of the best known and most capable officers of the Waffen-SS. Many started their career with the formation and later influenced other units, schools, and offices as their careers advanced. Even the most superficial reader of Waffen-SS books knows men such as Kurt "Panzer" Meyer, Max Wünsche, and Joachim Peiper. A few of the superlative officers of Sepp Dietrich's initial unit served their entire careers with the formation.

Among them is Theodor "Teddy" Wisch, the second officer to command the "Leibstandarte" and successor to Dietrich. The near obsessive interest in Sepp Dietrich and his iconic status seems to overshadow the later commanders of the formation historically. However, Wisch was not only a brave commander, but far exceeded Dietrich in training, tactician skills, and actual front line combat experience. He was famous long before the war while commanding the 1.Kompanie, which was often used as an elite guard for significant ceremonial functions. Wisch's natural abilities saw him rise through the ranks and become a full General in January 1944 without the benefit of officer school training. That deserved career rise saw him commanding a battalion and then a regiment prior to succeeding Dietrich. Typical of Waffen-SS officers, Wisch led his troops from the front and personally participated in combat at all command levels. His bravery, which caused all under him to obviously revere him, resulted in the award of the Knight's Cross with Oak Leaves and Swords, as well as the German Cross in Gold. Those awards also made him among the most decorated officers in the Waffen-SS.

After ten years of research centered on Theodor Wisch and the "Leibstandarte," Waffen-SS historian and author Mark C. Yerger approached me in the early summer of 2009, asking and motivating me to undertake the writing of a biography on this World War II military commander. Spontaneously accepting the challenge, since I believe that all information not shared is lost, I began work on the manuscript. I soon realized, however, that as an author I had an immense historical responsibility. Not only for the individual I was writing about but never met, but also for a generation of Germans.

By no means did I want to glorify or condemn, or blend in my own opinions, that could influence a neutral examination of this military commander. I believed that the reader would form his opinion, should he wish to, on a soldier influenced by the political, social, and economic circumstances of his times. I realized that in order to achieve this, I would need to focus on period documentation supported by the best postwar researched text material, and have done so to the best of my ability. These sources are noted throughout the text and bibliography.

It is important, however, that the reader bears in mind many contemporary texts reproduced in this book should be seen from the perspective of that period. Diary entries or comments made by individuals only represent the opinion of that person. So the author assumes the reader's common sense and logic when assimilating specific source material within their historical context.

Another question was to what extent the official unit history of the "Leibstandarte" was to be included. Many excellent works have already been written specifically on the unit's history throughout the years, including the aforementioned official five volume work written by Rudolf Lehmann and Ralf Tiemann. This study strictly focuses on Theodor Wisch. Having purchased a book on a specific commander, I'll assume a reader's basic knowledge regarding the division's history.

Detailed biographies on Sepp Dietrich, Wilhelm Mohnke, and Otto Kumm (three of the four "Leibstandarte" commanders) already exist in some format. It is my sincere wish that this work will close the final research gap of the formation's commanders in previously unavailable detail.

Having talked to and seen the eyes of many veterans during my years of studying World War II, it is inevitable not to fiercely condemn the act of war and its horrific consequences. May all future generations undertake every imaginable effort to maintain peace.

Markus Lippl
Spring 2011

THEODOR WISCH

Theodor Peter Johann Wisch was born December 13, 1907, in Wesselburener Koog, and was the son of farmer Theodor Wisch and his wife Berta (maiden name Martens). Wisch lived in one of Germany's most northern villages, in the province of Norderdithmarschen. He was the eldest of three brothers, all of whom would eventually serve within the "Leibstandarte."[1]

Frau Wisch died when Wisch was four, and after finishing his basic education during Easter 1923, he joined the "Jungstahlhelm" (Junior Stahlhelm) organization. That same year he began studying agriculture to emulate his father's vocation. After attending several schools for that field and working on several farms in East-Holstein and Holland, Wisch received his diploma in Schleswig as a certified agronomist in 1929.

Following World War I the economic times were difficult, and Wisch witnessed the closing of numerous farms in his home state. Impressed by the new National Socialist movement of Adolf Hitler, Wisch became a member of the NSDAP (Party# 369 050) on November 1, 1930, and joined the SS the following day (SS# 4 759).[2]

Serving as an SS-Mann in the 53.SS-Standarte in Wesselburen, he was promoted to SS-Scharführer on March 1, 1931, and became a SS-Truppführer on January 8, 1932.[3] That same year he was convicted of bodily injury after a confrontation with communists and sentenced to six months in prison.[4] On February 17, 1931, and October 17, 1932, Wisch took part in marches in Braunschweig, and also participated in the Reichsjugendtreffen (Reichs Youth Meeting) in Potsdam on October 8, 1932.[5] Wisch led the 1./I./53.SS-Standarte from October 1932 to March 1933.

In February 1933, soon after Hitler was elected chancellor, SS-Gruppenführer Josef "Sepp" Dietrich visited various SS Standarten, especially in Northern Germany.[6] He personally

[1] Fritz Wisch joined the SS-Sonderkommando Jüterbog in August 1934, finally serving as an SS-Oberscharführer with the 17./ IV./LSSAH in 1941. Hans J. Wisch enlisted in the SS-Sonderkommando Zossen in May 1933 and was an SS-Oberscharführer when killed in action near Nürnberg on April 24, 1945.

[2] Partybook (1930-1936) of Theodor Wisch, see illustration.

[3] The headquarters of 53.SS-Standarte was moved to Heide/Holstein after 1937.

[4] Spruchgericht, 13.Spruchkammer, AZ: 9 Sp.Ls. 136/48 – 13/37; Spruchgerichtsverfahren gegen den SS-Brigadeführer und Generalmajor der Waffen-SS Theodor Wisch, Sitzung vom 08.03.1948.

[5] Partybook (1930-1936) of Theodor Wisch, page 22, handwritten entry by SS-Sturmhauptführer Herwig, 53.SS-Standarte, see illustration.

[6] Dietrich was born on May 28, 1892, in Hawangen. Finishing school at 16 in Memmingen, he worked as a horse carriage driver and waiter in Holland, Austria, and Italia. During 1909 to 1911 he was a hotel clerk in Switzerland and a butcher in Munich. Dietrich joined the 2./7.Bayerische Feldartillerie Regiment "König" by mid-October 1911, being discharged a month later following an accident. He was then a bakery delivery man in Memmingen. Drafted into the 7.Bayerische Feldartillerie Regiment on August 6, 1914, he transferred to the 6.Bayerische Reserve-Feldartillerie-Regiment in October that year. After being wounded Dietrich took an artillery school course in Sonthofen in January 1915. He served with artillery and infantry units until February 18, 1918, then became a gunner with the Bayerische Sturmpanzerkampfwagen Abteilung 13 until November 20, 1918. Returning to Artillerie Regiment "Prinzregent Luitpold," he won both classes of the Iron Cross, the Tank Battle Badge in Silver, and the Wound Badge in Black, as well as Bavarian and Austrian decorations. Discharged on March 26, 1919, as a Vizewachtmeister, he moved to Munich and joined the Bavarian Landespolizei on October 1, 1919. Commissioned in October 1919, Dietrich was promoted to Oberleutnant in 1923 and to Hauptmann in 1924. Taking a leave of absence, he fought with the Freikorps "Oberland" in Upper Silesia and participated in the November 9, 1923, Munich Putsch (awarded Blood Order #10). Employed as a garage manager at the Blau-Bock gas station among other jobs, including the customs service, Dietrich joined the NSDAP on May 1, 1928, and the SS four days later. Commissioned on June 1, 1928, he led the eventual 1.SS-Standarte in Munich from August 1, 1928, to September 18, 1929, being promoted to Standartenführer on November 18, 1929. He also worked as a Franz-Eher publishing house packer in Munich. During September 19, 1929, to July 11, 1930, Dietrich led SS-Brigade "Bayern" and was Gau SS Leader of Munich-Upper Bavaria. Promoted to Oberführer on July 11, 1930, he was SS-Oberführer Süd (Munich) from July 11, 1930, to August 14, 1931. During August 14, 1931, to October 1, 1932, Dietrich led SS-Abschnitt IV "Nord" (Brunswick), being promoted to Gruppenführer on December 18th that year. He commanded Hitler's bodyguard unit, the Begleitkommando "Der Führer," from February 1932 to March 17th the next year and led SS-Gruppe "Nord" (Hamburg) from October 1932 into March 1933. From March 17 to August 2, 1933, he commanded the Stabswache Berlin, which became the "Adolf-Hitler-Standarte" in October 1933 and progressively the "Leibstandarte," which he continued to lead. On July 11, 1933, Dietrich was elected Preussischer Staatsrat and formally led SS Oberabschnitt "Ost" (Berlin) from October 1, 1933, to the end of the war. Commanding the "Leibstandarte," he participated in the Röhm Putsch from June 30 to July 1, 1934, and became an Obergruppenführer on July 1, 1934. See photo caption and footnote 39.

selected eligible men which would eventually form the newly created "SS-Stabswache Berlin." The unit later developed into the "Leibstandarte." Theodor Wisch was among the first 117 men selected to join the "SS-Stabswache Berlin" on March 17, 1933. They can be regarded as partial cadre of the SS-Verfügungstruppe that later became the Waffen-SS.[7] Among the "First 120," as they called themselves, were men such as later divisional commanders Fritz Witt and Wilhelm Mohnke, as well as other future regimental, battalion, and company commanders of the Waffen-SS.

After serving as a platoon leader for four months in Berlin, Wisch, along with three Unterführer (NCOs) and 24 men under his command, were ordered to serve as the first Wachkommando at Hitler's "Haus Wachenfeld," at the Obersalzberg near Berchtesgaden. That assignment lasted from 1 July until the beginning of October that year.[8]

Having been commissioned a Sturmführer on June 28, 1933, Wisch was ordered to interrupt his duty at the Berghof to participate in the fifth Party Rally at Nürnberg during August 31 to September 3, 1933. There the unit was officially named the Leibstandarte SS "Adolf Hitler," receiving its well-known unit colors. Additionally, all members of the Standarte thereafter were allowed to wear the name "Adolf Hitler" on a cufftitle sewn to their lower left tunic sleeve. Promoted to Sturmhauptführer on October 1, 1933, and having returned to the Reichshauptstadt Berlin, Wisch was appointed commander of the 1.Kompanie of the Leibstandarte SS "Adolf Hitler" on October 7, 1933. He lead his proud 1.Kompanie one month later in Munich at the "March of the Old Fighters," the inauguration of the memorial next to the Feldherrnhalle, where they swore their oath to Reichskanzler Adolf Hitler. On May 29, 1934, Wisch was given permission to wear the honor dagger after having been a member of the SS since November 1930.[9]

The 1.Kompanie "Die Erste" (The First), as it was called by its men, earned fame during the ensuing prewar years as Germany's premier parade, ceremonial, and guards unit. The unit was present at almost every important political and cultural event in Germany. Some of these were the following:

August 7, 1934: Funeral ceremony at the National Tannenberg-Memorial in honor of Reichspräsident Paul von Hindenburg's death on August 2, 1934.

March 1, 1935: Return of the Saarland from French occupation to Germany.

February 6, 1936: Opening ceremony of the XI.Olympic Winter Games in Garmisch-Partenkirchen.

August 1, 1936: Opening events of the XI. Olympic Summer Games in Berlin.

September 25-29, 1937: Visit of Benito Mussolini to Munich and Berlin.

March 15, 1938: Parade in Vienna after the annexation of Austria.

But the "Leibstandarte" also continued its military development throughout these years. As part of his early officer training, Wisch was ordered to participate in an infantry leadership training course at the Army's Infantry School at Döberitz from July 2 to August 28, 1935. During this eight week training course he showed severe insecurity during the course, since he lacked basic military skills. School commandant Oberstleutnant Hans Hube evaluated him as unqualified to lead an infantry platoon.[10] In a letter to Himmler on November 11, 1935, later Diamonds to the Knight's Cross winner Hube wrote:

> "Hauptsturmführer Wisch, proved himself to be a very valuable and soldierly personality, enjoying a very high respect amongst all instructors of the infantry school. However, his infantry leadership skills were so little that, judged by his military knowledge, he does not seem suitable as a company commander. Since he lacked practice as an infantry NCO, during small combat training sessions (the daily bread of a combat instructor) he is very insecure and unskilled. During the eight weeks of the course's duration, it was impossible to eliminate his weaknesses due to that missing knowledge. Wisch is however able to develop and will certainly acquire the necessary skills for being a platoon or company leader with continuing practice."[11]

[7] Partybook (1930-1936) of Theodor Wisch, page 23. Handwritten entry by SS-Gruppenführer Dietrich, see illustration.

[8] "Haus Wachenfeld" was purchased by Hitler in 1933. Refurbished and largely expanded, it was renamed the "Berghof" in 1935/1936.

[9] Partybook (1930-1936) of Theodor Wisch, page 24, Entry stamped "Leibstandarte Adolf Hitler" and signed by Sturmhauptführer Leroix, see illustration.

[10] Hans-Valentin Hube (October 29, 1890-April 20, 1944) died in a fatal plane crash as Generaloberst and Commander of the 1.Panzer-Armee while returning from his Diamonds award ceremony at Hitler's Berghof.

[11] Personalakte Theodor Wisch, Letter from Oberstleutnant und Kommander der Infanterie Schule Hube to Himmler dated November 28, 1935.

On November 5, 1935, Wisch officially signed his enlistment contract as an officer of the SS-Verfügungstruppe, binding him contractually to service until age 45.[12] He married his wife Sigrid Hanna Mühlenhardt in Hamburg on November 27, 1936, and their first son, Klaus Peter, was born on 17 October the following year.[13] From January 17 to January 28, 1938, Wisch took part in a training course held at the Heeressportschule (Army Sports School) at Wünsdorf.[14] In March and October 1938 he participated in the annexation of Austria and Czechoslovakia, earning both commemorative campaign medals to include the "Prague Castle" clasp. On February 21, 1939, his son Reimer Johann was born.

When German forces crossed Poland's border in the early morning hours of September 1, 1939, Wisch led his company into combat for the first time. They received their baptism of fire engaging Polish forces in Pabianice, Warsaw, and around the Bzura River, until successfully ending operations near Modlin on September 27, 1939. For his bravery and leadership, Generalleutnant Georg-Hans Reinhardt, commander of the Army's 4.Panzer-Divison, awarded Wisch both classes of the Iron Cross on September 24 and November 8, 1939.[15]

> "In Poland we experienced our baptism of fire side-by-side with our former company commander, SS-Hauptsturmführer Wisch. He laid beside us in the trenches with the iron calmness of a northern German farmer's son. He always led his company from the front during the victorious days of the Polish campaign. He was more than a leader of a company; he was a comrade and advisor to his men with all their worries. One normally claims the "Spiess" (Staff Sergeant) is the mother of the company. Commander Wisch was the father of all the men who had served in his company throughout the years. He knew them all, their needs and weaknesses, but also knew their loyalty and enthusiasm."[16]

The previous quotation shows why Wisch was, especially to his longer serving men, known as and often referred to as "Teddy," expressing their affection for him as their commander. After some well earned weeks of rest, Obergruppenführer Dietrich proposed Wisch's promotion to Sturmbannführer on January 4, 1940, requesting at the same time he get command of the newly created IV.(Wach) Battalion in Berlin-Lichterfelde. Those requests were approved by Himmler, and Wisch was formally promoted to Sturmbannführer on January 30, 1940.[17] His successor was Obersturmführer Martin Gross, previously a platoon leader in Wisch's 1.Kompanie.

The IV.(Wach) Battalion staff in Berlin-Lichterfelde was structured as follows during the time Wisch was in command of the unit:

Kommandeur:	Sturmbannführer Theodor Wisch
Adjutant:	Obersturmführer Günter Hausdorf
Ordonnanzoffizier:	Untersturmführer Karl Döring
Battalionsarzt (Doctor):	Hauptsturmführer Dr. Friedrich Winne
Technischer Führer K(I):	Obersturmführer Adolf Petersen
Verwaltungsführer:	Hauptsturmführer Max Müller

Wisch's departure from the 1./Leibstandarte was a sentimental moment, especially for the longer serving men who had followed their respected commander through the peacetime years of the "Leibstandarte." But his loyal comrades knew that his skills and experience were vitally needed for the further growth of their unit and the challenges that waited ahead.

The new battalion commander went to work immediately. Training of the recruits was carried out in the areas surrounding Berlin, and regularly in the southern courtyard

[12] "Dienstvertrag", Personalakte Theodor Wisch.

[13] Personalakte Theodor Wisch, Lebenslauf written while a Brigadeführer. The marriage is registered at Standesamt Hamburg-Eimsbüttel (formerly Standesamt 20b), under reference 261/1936. (Information Mrs. Nadine Schäfer, Generalregister der hamburger Standesämter dated October 13, 2009). Frau Mühlenhardt was the daughter of an interior decorator.

[14] Personalakte Theodor Wisch, Dienstlaufbahn des Theodor Wisch, 1945.

[15] Georg-Hans Reinhardt (March 01, 1887-November 24, 1963) was awarded the Swords to the Knight's Cross on May 26, 1944, as a Generaloberst commanding Heeresgruppe "Nord." In January 1945 he was placed in reserve following disputes with Hitler.

[16] SS-Kriegsberichter (War Reporter) Günther Honolka, "Das Schwarze Korps" issue of October 1, 1941.

[17] Personalakte Theodor Wisch, "Beförderungen in der Waffen-SS."

of the "Leibstandarte" barracks in Berlin-Lichterfelde. Wisch frequently paid the new training companies a visit to personally influence the progress his units were making.

Günther Borchers, a later Untersturmführer and platoon leader in the "Leibstandarte" Panzer Regiment, recalled:

> "Through disciplined and tough training we had been made a solid unit. And that was to be proven during future battles. We wanted to be sent to the front! Our battalion commander Sturmbannführer Wisch was often present during our training. Then our NCOs were immediately quieter. Still we sweat sufficiently."[18]

By the end of May 1941, Wisch was given command of the second battalion of the now expanded "Leibstandarte," succeeding Sturmbannführer Erwin Horstmann. On June 22, 1941, Operation "Barbarossa" commenced, the campaign against the Soviet Union. As part of Generalfeldmarschall Ewald von Kleist's Panzer Gruppe 1, the "Leibstandarte" moved into action with the objective to capture the Ukrainian capital of Kiev.[19]

In July 1941, having in the meantime been given command of the second battalion of the now expanded "Leibstandarte," Wisch and his men were involved in fierce combat for days at the Rollbahn "Nord" (Northern transport road), west of Shitomir, near Sokolov. Between 11 and 17 July they fought back 36 heavy Russian attacks, securing the vitally important transport route for Panzer Gruppe 1. On one of these difficult days, realizing that a motorcycle battalion of the Army was threatened by total annihilation, Wisch spontaneously decided to mobilize his battalion and counter attack the much stronger Russian enemy. As a result of this spontaneous action he successfully saved this Army unit from complete destruction.[20]

But even though Wisch had achieved a significant success, while leading his men in this difficult week of combat day and night there was also a high personal price paid: his younger brother Fritz, an Oberscharführer with the 17./ IV./Leibstandarte, had fallen during an attack on the village of Henrykowka on July 13, 1941.[21] Having been wounded on July 28, 1941, Wisch stayed with his battalion and continued the advance towards Uman.

Two months later the "Leibstandarte" had moved further south and separated into two groups. Group "East," directly led by Obergruppenführer Dietrich, advanced against the Crimean peninsula. Group "West," led by Obersturmbannführer Wilhelm Keilhaus, consisting of the reinforced II. and IV. battalions and the "Leibstandarte" engineer battalion, moved against the Liman peninsula.[22] It was there in the early morning hours of September 19, 1941, during heavy fighting against Soviet Army and Navy forces, that a special radio message reached Wisch at his command post that read as follows:

> "The Führer and Supreme Commander of the Wehrmacht has awarded the Knight's Cross of the Iron Cross to SS-Sturmbannführer Wisch, Kdr. II./ LSSAH on Sept.15. Award certificate and decoration to follow by courier. Panzergruppe 1/ IIa".[23]

Untersturmführer Josef Diefenthal, Wisch's battalion adjutant (IIa), reported the very special moment:

> "The adjutant swings himself onto the motorcycle and is gone. A quick drive to the communication post, to see whether there is anything new. The leader of the communication troop, barely able to speak a word, has a radio message in his hand and mumbles something about the commander and a Knight's Cross. Laughs, cries and does not know what is going on himself. And now the adjutant. Give me the message, onto the motorcycle and back. After an involuntarily roll he lands, still split seconds

[18] Personal diary of SS-Untersturmführer Günther Borchers, SS-Panzer-Regiment 1. Original in collection of the author.

[19] Ewald von Kleist (August 18, 1881-November 13, 1954) was awarded the Swords to the Knight's Cross on March 30, 1944. Promoted to Generalfeldmarschall on February 1, 1943, he was the last commander of Heeresgruppe "A." Arrested by the Gestapo in connection with the failed plot against Hitler on July 20, 1944, but later released, he died at the Wladimirowka POW camp in Russia.

[20] Personalakte Theodor Wisch, "Vorschlagsliste zur Verleihung des Eichenlaubs" dated February 8, 1944, and signed SS-Obergruppenführer und Panzergeneral der Waffen-SS Dietrich as commander of Generalkommando I.SS-Panzer-Korps "Leibstandarte SS Adolf Hitler."

[21] According to information from the Wisch family, Theodor Wisch personally evacuated his brother under enemy fire from the battlefield.

[22] Wilhelm Keilhaus (December 11, 1898-January 10, 1977) was awarded the German Cross in Gold on April 29, 1942, as Ia of the LSSAH, Promoted to Brigadeführer and Generalmajor der Waffen-SS on April 20, 1944, he became the Inspector of Inspectorate 7 (Signal Troops). Keilhaus was also chief of telecommunications of the Reichsführer-SS and Minister of the Interior, Heinrich Himmler.

[23] Original radio message to SS-Sturmbannführer Wisch dated September 19, 1941, see illustration. Original in the collection of the author.

faster than a Russian Flak-grenade, next to the commander: 'Sturmbannführer, may I congratulate you to the Knight's Cross?'-'What's going on? Don't make jokes!' And continuously more Flak-grenades howl and scream over our heads. The radio message convinces him after some time and during the initial joy the noise of the battle is being forgotten. Quickly an Iron Cross Second Class is converted and attached to his collar in a ceremonial manner. An unbelievable feeling for everyone who had been there. Through this high award, a gigantic five day battle in July against a complete Russian Army at the Rollbahn 'Nord,' brings the commander and his exceptional battalion the well earned recognition and a worthy ending."[24]

Days later, in the evening hours of September 27, 1941, Wisch received a telegram from Reichsführer-SS Heinrich Himmler, congratulating him on the award of the Knight's Cross and at the same time notifying him about his promotion to Obersturmbannführer. The following months the II./ Leibstandarte saw further heavy action in the southeastern Ukraine, north of the Sea of Azov, advancing through Mariupol and Taganrog towards the city of Rostov, which was consequently captured on November 21, 1941.

But the victory achieved at Rostov would not last long. The Oberkommando der Wehrmacht underestimated the strength of the Russians. They failed to supply the troops with sufficient winter clothing or equipment to maintain their vehicles operating in temperatures as low as minus 25°C.

The city was held for a little more than a month before the Division was forced to abandon it in a swift move back east just over the Mius river to Ssambek on December 1, 1941. There a defensive line was established to withstand the enormous pressure of Russian forces pushing west. A fierce struggle over this line began to unfold over the winter months and well into the following year, during which the enemy was unable to break through the "Leibstandarte" lines. Dietrich later wrote of Wisch's conduct throughout the months of fighting:

"In the further battles of the Eastern Campaign 1941, especially during the cleaning of the Nogai Steppe in September 1941, the capture of Mariupol, and the defensive battles in and westwards Rostov, the leadership skills and personal bravery of SS-Brigadeführer Wisch have repeatedly been proven. His battalion was widely separated from the Division and frequently operating independently without any contact. With a highly developed instinct for the weaknesses of the enemy, often after personal reconnaissance in the foremost line, he accomplished the assignments of the Division. In doing so he achieved great success in the tactical sense, as well as in the destruction of tremendous quantities of men and material."[25]

Amidst the heavy fighting, news reached Wisch that his wife had given birth to their first daughter, Maren, on February 20, 1942. After having been awarded the Infantry Assault Badge in Bronze on March 2, 1942, Theodor Wisch was forced to leave his battalion by the end of the month. Due to thrombosis in his left foot he had to undergo treatment at the SS hospital in Berlin.[26] The "Leibstandarte" continued defending the Mius line under catastrophic climatic conditions, and was finally relieved by Sicherungs-Regiment 4, Polizei-Regiment z.b.V., and the 5.Romanian Cavalry Division on June 1, 1942.

In June, while providing coastal defense in the Stalino-Mariupol area, the "Leibstandarte" was re-named SS-Division Leibstandarte-SS "Adolf Hitler". It was refitted and formally reorganized into two infantry regiments on July 5, 1942. The staff of Wisch's SS-Infanterie-Regiment 2 was organized as follows:

Kommandeur:	Standartenführer Theodor Wisch
IIa (Adjutant):	Obersturmführer Josef Diefenthal
Ordonnanzoffizier:	Untersturmführer Otto Günsche
z.b.V. (Special Duties Officer):	Hauptsturmführer Artur Klingemeier
IVa (Administration):	Hauptsturmführer Heinz Lange
IVb (Doctor):	Hauptsturmführer Dr. Hellmut Vieweg
Zahnarzt (Dentist):	Untersturmführer Dr. Alfred Schmitt
V (Technical Officer):	Sturmbannführer Georg Stoltz
Chef Stabskompanie:	Obersturmführer Siegfried Wandt
TFW (Technical Officer Weapons):	Untersturmführer Oskar Röntgen

[24] Report written by SS-Untersturmführer Josef "Jupp" Diefenthal dated September 19, 1941, "Die Leibstandarte" by Rudolf Lehmann, Volume II, 1980. During a later official ceremony, Dietrich presented Wisch with a formal Knight's Cross award.

(Footnotes 25 and 26 see p 12)

On July 10, 1942, the Division was ordered to France and assembled in an area southeast of Paris. Wisch, fully recovered from his March illness, rejoined the Division and was officially given command of SS-Infanterie-Regiment 2 in August 1942. The following months were being used to train and refresh the Division. It was continuously put on alarm status due to constant threats of an allied invasion, such as the Canadian attempt at Dieppe in the early morning hours of August 19, 1942. The "Leibstandarte" was expended with the addition of a Panzer Regiment by mid-October and renamed SS-Panzer-Grenadier-Division "Leibstandarte SS Adolf Hitler" two months later. SS-Infanterie-Regiment 2 accordingly had its designation changed to SS-Panzer-Grenadier-Regiment 2 and its III.Batallion, commanded by Sturmbannführer Joachim Peiper, was refitted with armored personnel carriers.

On December 13, 1942, Wisch celebrated his 32nd birthday with his comrades, who on the occasion presented him with a book on "Frederic the Great" that was signed by some of his regimental staff members. Passing some quiet Christmas days in France, the division was suddenly struck by a mobilization order on December 30, 1942, ordering its immediate deployment to the East. The same day the SS-Führungshauptamt (Leadership Main Office) ordered Wisch's participation in a regimental leadership training course, to be held at the Army's Panzertruppenschule (Armored Troop School) Wünsdorf during January 4, 1943, to January 25, 1943.[27]

After the complete surrender of the German forces at Stalingrad, the Soviet Supreme Command aimed to cut off and destroy German Army Group "South." Being led by Generalfeldmarschall Erich von Manstein, the Russian objective made a new deployment of the "Leibstandarte," alongside its sister divisions "Das Reich" and "Totenkopf," into the Ukraine necessary. The three divisions formed the SS-Panzer Korps, commanded by Obergruppenführer und General der Waffen-SS Paul "Papa" Hausser.[28] Effective January 30, 1943, Wisch was promoted to the rank of Standartenführer.[29] In his request for the promotion Obergruppenführer Dietrich wrote:

> "With the beginning of the Russian campaign, Wisch took over command of the II.Batallion and has participated exceptionally well in all battles. He distinguished himself through with initiative, circumspection, and personal bravery in front of the enemy and was decorated with the Knight's Cross. His character is outstanding. Wisch is extraordinarily liked by the officers, NCOs and men. During his duty in the Standarte he earned my full satisfaction. Wisch is now leading the SS-Infanterie-Regiment 2. I consider Wisch quite suitable for promotion to SS-Standartenführer."[30]

---

[25] "Vorschlagsliste für die Verleihung des Eichenlaubs" dated February 8, 1944, signed SS-Obergruppenführer und Panzergeneral der Waffen-SS Josef Dietrich. Generalkommando I.SS-Panzer-Korps "Leibstandarte SS Adolf Hitler." Note that Dietrich refers to Wisch as "SS-Brigadeführer" in this 1944 dated document while he was a SS-Sturmbannführer and SS-Obersturmbannführer during the combats described.

[26] Personalakte Theodor Wisch.

[27] Personalakte Theodor Wisch, Personalverfügung, SS-FHA Berlin-Wilmersdorf December 30, 1942.

[28] Paul Hausser was born on October 7, 1880, in Brandenburg an der Havel and joined the Prussian cadet corps in Köslin, later moving to Berlin-Lichterfelde. Commissioned on March 18, 1899, Hausser served as a battalion and regimental adjutant with the 7.(Westpreussiches) Infanterie Regiment Nr. 155 until 1907. Next attending the Kriegsakademie in Posen until 1909, he was then an aerial observer with the Kriegsmarine until 1912. Promoted to Oberleutnant in 1912, Hausser served in the Greater General Staff from March 1913 and then with Crown Prince Rupprecht of Bavaria's staff, becoming a Hauptmann i.G. on October 1, 1913. With the outbreak of WWI, he was posted to the 6.Armeekorps and was Ia of the 109.Infanterie Division. Promoted to Major in 1919, Hausser was Ia of the I.Reserve Korps and commanded Fusilier Regiment "Generalfeldmarschall Graf Moltke" (Schlesisches) Nr. 88. He won both Classes of the Iron Cross in WWI, as well as numerous other military and state awards. From January 1, 1921, Hausser was the first Ia of the 2.Division, being promoted to Oberstleutnant on November 15, 1922. He then commanded the III./Infanterie Regiment 4 (2.Division) from 1923 to April 1925 before becoming Chief of Staff of the 2.Division. In January 1927 Hausser was attached to the staff of Infanterie Regiment 10, later commanding the regiment and being promoted to Oberst on November 1, 1927. From November 1930 to February 1932 he was Infanterieführer for the Fourth Military District, and while there was promoted to Generalmajor on February 1, 1931. Retiring as a Generalleutnant at the end of January 1932, he joined the Stahlhelm in Berlin-Brandenburg in February 1933. When the Stahlhelm was absorbed by the SA he became an SA-Standartenführer on March 5, 1934, with SA Reserve Brigade 25. Invited by Himmler to train the SS-Verfügungstruppe, he joined the SS as a Standartenführer on November 15, 1934, and was the first commander of SS-Führerschule Braunschweig until June 1, 1936. Promoted to Oberführer on July 1, 1935, and to Brigadeführer on May 22, 1936, Hausser was Chief of Staff of the Führungsamt from June 1936. Hausser held the post of Inspektor der SS-Junkerschulen (August 1, 1935, to May 1, 1937), and also became Inspektor der SS-Verfügungstruppe (October 1, 1936, to August 1939). Additionally, he headed the Führungsamt within the SS-Hauptamt during May 1936 to October 1937. Having joined the NSDAP on May 1, 1937, Hausser became a Gruppenführer on June 1, 1939 (see photo section).

[29] Original Promotion document dated January 30, 1943, signed by Reichsführer-SS Heinrich Himmler, see illustration. Original in collection of the author.

[30] Personalakte Theodor Wisch "Beförderungen in der Waffen-SS," dated August 5, 1942.

Wisch and the staff of SS-Panzer-Grenadier-Regiment 2 arrived in Tschugujew, at the southeast of Kharkov, on February 2, 1943. The regiment immediately initiated the building of defensive positions together with the help of civilians. It was not until three days later that the regiment felt the full thrust of the Russian troops starting attacks on the unit's positions.

Ten days of fierce combat followed, with the Regiment slowly being pushed back west over the Donez river by enemy forces ten times stronger. On February 15th Obergruppenführer Paul Hausser saw no option but to evacuate Kharkov against Adolf Hitler's direct order. This was done in order to prevent encirclement and the complete annihilation of the troops under his command. One day after Hausser's crucial order, during the ongoing decisive battles south of Kharkov, Obergruppenführer Dietrich requested the award of the German Cross in Gold for Wisch. It was approved and formally awarded on February 25, 1943.

Wisch was one of less than 850 soldiers of the Waffen-SS who earned the prestigious Order, awarded for multiple acts of personal bravery and leadership in the field.[31] Unfortunately, the detailed recommendation document did not survive. Based on a draft recommendation signed by Dietrich, it can be assumed that Wisch's leadership in the following battles contributed to his award:

Battle near Uman, Defensive battles near Sokolowka between July 27-30, 1941.
Defensive battles near Nowo-Archangesk between August 1-8, 1941.
Capture of Cherson on August 18, 1941.
Destruction of Russian Forces on the peninsula south of the Dnepr-Delta between September 12-21, 1941.
Defensive battles at the Don (Rostov) from November 22-29, 1941.
Defensive battles during the winter of 1941/42 in the Ssambek area east of Taganrog.
Defensive battles east of Kharkov, February 1-15, 1943.[32]

The battles between the Donez and Dnepr rivers continued. By the beginning of March the enemy attack lost momentum in their advance to the south due to supply constraints and heavy casualties. By the fifth of the month the 1.SS-Panzer-Grenadier Division "Leibstandarte," together with the 2.SS-Panzer-Grenadier-Division "Das Reich" and the 3.SS-Panzer-Grenadier-Division "Totenkopf," began a counterattack north towards Kharkov. Within five days the "Leibstandarte" had advanced powerfully, with Wisch and his regiment standing in the town of Dergatschi, only twelve kilometers north of the city's center. Obergruppenführer Dietrich wrote the following summary of Wisch's actions during the Kharkov operations:

> "In the winter campaign of February/March 1943 as commander of SS-Panzer-Grenadier Regiment 2 'LSSAH', SS-Brigadeführer Wisch has again proven himself as a leader and champion for is men. Under his personal leadership, in the thinly occupied security line east of Kharkov and the ordered disengagement movement of his regiment, he and his men were able to fight off all massive Russian assaults. He succeeded in picking up the 298th and 320th Infantry Divisions from the foreground of the main battle line, as well as considerably weakening the enemy forces with a counterattack of his III. Battalion.
>
> The counterattack started on March 2, 1943, and was personally led by SS-Brigadeführer Wisch. With the most forward companies and his armored III.Battalion he took Bf. Ljachowa and forced a bridgehead at Bridok. In doing so he created the conditions for the capture of Walki. Again under his personal leadership, SS-Brigadeführer Wisch was able to take Ogulzy and Ljabotin, the starting point for the attack on Kharkov. During the battles for Kharkov, operating with his regiment on the right open flank, he was able to penetrate the railway installations during the first day of combat on March 10, 1943. From there the city center was taken and two days later the eastern part of Kharkov after they'd eliminated the threat on their flank from the higher situated and, intensively wooden southern part of Kharkov."[33]

Sturmmann Günther Borchers, an engineer in the 5./SS-Panzer-Grenadier-Regiment 2, kept a diary of his experiences at that time. Regarding the attack on the city on March 13th he wrote:

> "Early in the morning the fighting continues. The company suffers heavy losses. Fierce battles are raging. The Russian is defending his positions

[31] During the war slightly over 24,000 soldiers of all service branches were awarded with the German Cross in Gold.

[32] "Vorschlag für die Verleihung des Deutschen Kreuzes in Gold," dated February 15, 1943, and signed SS-Obergruppenführer und General der Waffen-SS Dietrich.

[33] "Vorschlagsliste für die Verleihung des Eichenlaubs" dated February 8, 1944, signed SS-Obergruppenführer und Panzergeneral der Waffen-SS Dietrich. Generalkommando I.SS-Panzerkorps "Leibstandarte SS Adolf Hitler."

persistently. We attack forcefully. Frequently the cannons have to enter the street fighting and finish with the houses in direct fire (100 meters or less). But the Russian keeps on firing out of the cellars of the destroyed houses. I receive a number of shots into my sidecar. Transverse shots zoom through the streets. A grenade rips the motorcycle driving in front of me to pieces. I took a splinter in my knee and a couple of more into my bike. But my machine keeps on rolling. Sturmbannführer Hansen (1.Regiment) took the 'Red Square'. Out of the side streets and gardens more and more T-34s engage in the fighting against us. Everywhere are Stalin figures made from gypsum. We stick to the Russian and attack him, wherever he shows himself. So we fight from house to house, street to street through Kharkov. The 'Red Square' is being renamed 'Square of the 'Leibstandarte.'"[34]

Obergruppenführer Dietrich continued summarizing Wisch's leadership of SS-Panzer-Grenadier-Regiment 2. He wrote after the fierce fighting for Kharkov as follows:

"The surprise capture of Bjelgorod in March 1943 was begun by powerful attacks of his regiment, which he personally led from the front lines once again. They were executed after breaking the initial fierce resistance, prepared by a wide area pursuit, and carried out ideally in all important moments through his personal issuing of orders to the III. Battalion of his regiment."[35]

With the City of Kharkov taken back into German possession on March 14, 1943, and the capture of Belgorod, the "Leibstandarte" went into a time of rest, refitting, and restructuring. Wisch's SS-Panzer-Grenadier-Regiment 2 alone had suffered the following losses during the recapture of Kharkov: [36]

	Officers	NCOs	Enlisted men
Killed:	14	54	239
Wounded:	30	143	615
Missing:	1	6	34
Sick/Accidents:	2	14	304
Total:	47	217	1192

Following a meeting between Obergruppenführer Dietrich and Adolf Hitler in May 1943, the formation of the I.SS-Panzer-Korps "Leibstandarte" was ordered. It included the commissioning of a new division, the 12.SS-Panzer-Grenadier-Division "Hitlerjugend." It was led by Standartenführer Fritz Witt, who had been succeeded by Obersturmbannführer Albert Frey as the commander of SS-Panzer-Grenadier-Regiment 1.[37] Other "Leibstandarte" leadership cadre personnel for this sister unit included Max Wünsche, Wilhelm Mohnke, and Kurt "Panzer" Meyer.[38]

Dietrich was to assume command of the new I.SS-Panzer-Korps, and it was Wisch whom he appointed as his

[34] Personal diary of SS-Untersturmführer Günther Borchers SS-Panzer-Regiment 1 "LSSAH." Original in collection of the author.

[35] "Vorschlagsliste für die Verleihung des Eichenlaubs" dated February 8, 1944, and signed SS-Obergruppenführer und Panzergeneral der Waffen-SS Dietrich. Generalkommando I.SS-Panzerkorps "Leibstandarte SS Adolf Hitler."

[36] "Die Leibstandarte" by Rudolf Lehmann, Volume III, 1982.

[37] A prewar graduate of Junkerschule Braunschweig, Albert Frey was commissioned on March 19, 1938. He won the German Cross in Gold as a Hauptsturmführer on November 17, 1941, as commander of the III./Infanterie Regiment (mot.) "LSSAH." Promoted to Sturmbannführer on March 20, 1942, Frey then won the Knight's Cross on March 3, 1943, for leading the I./SS-Panzer-Grenadier-Regiment 1. Having been promoted to Obersturmbannführer on July 5, 1943, his command of SS-Panzer-Grenadier Regiment 1 west of Kiev along the "Shitomir-Kiev" rail line won him the Oakleaves on December 29, 1943, following a recommendation by Theodor Wisch. Promoted to Standartenführer on August 1, 1944, he and his wife died in Heilbronn on September 1, 2003.

[38] Kurt "Panzer" Meyer (SS #17 559) was born on December 23, 1910, in Jerxheim. He entered the Allgemeine-SS on October 15, 1931, and the "Leibstandarte" on May 15, 1934. Commissioned on July 10, 1932, he was promoted to Obersturmführer on March 10, 1935. Meyer headed the 14.(Panzerabwehr)/Kompanie "Leibstandarte" from September 1935 and was promoted to Hauptsturmführer on September 12, 1937. After leading the 14.Kompanie in Poland he became commander of the 15.(Kradschützen)/Kompanie that eventually expanded into the "Leibstandarte" reconnaissance detachment. As reconnaissance commander he became a Sturmbannführer on September 1, 1940. During Operation Barbarossa he won the Knight's Cross on May 18, 1941, and the German Cross in Gold on February 8, 1942. Promoted to Obersturmbannführer on November 9, 1942, on February 23, 1943, Meyer won the Oakleaves to the Knight's Cross. Next promoted to Standartenführer on June 21, 1943, he became the first commander of SS-Panzer-Grenadier-Regiment 25 of the new 12.SS-Panzer-Division "Hitlerjugend." After the death of Brigadeführer Fritz Witt on June 14, 1944, Meyer became commander of "Hitlerjugend" and won the Swords to the Knight's Cross for that command on August 27, 1944, followed by promotion to Brigadeführer on September 1, 1944. He was captured by Belgian partisans near Liege on September 6, 1944, and consequently handed over to the British for trial. His death sentence was commuted and he was released from prison in the fall of 1954. Kurt Meyer died from a heart attack on his birthday in 1961.

successor to command the SS-Panzer-Grenadier-Division "Leibstandarte SS Adolf Hitler."[39] As Wisch's successor, Sturmbannführer and Knight's Cross holder Hugo Kraas took command of SS-Panzer-Grenadier-Regiment 2. Even though he was formally to assume command of the Division on July 4, 1943, for practicality reasons Wisch and his staff were already worked into their new positions by the end of May.

Wisch faced no easy task in taking over the position as commander of the "Leibstandarte." He was to lead a division which was much focused on the charismatic personality of Dietrich, who had created and led the unit for more than ten years. Nevertheless, Wisch immediately managed to transfer the support he had enjoyed from his Regiment to the Division. Obersturmführer Erhard Gührs, the adjutant of Peiper's III.(gep.)/SS-Panzer-Grenadier-Regiment 2, recalled:

> "Teddy Wisch always had an excellent reputation in our division. He was honest, sincere, and a rational commander. He did a great job taking over the division!"[40]

Brigadeführer and Swords holder Otto Kumm, the last commander of the "Leibstandarte," commented many years later in a personal meeting with the author that Wisch was "a fabulous commander, whom he liked a lot!"[41] Likewise, Oberscharführer and Knight's Cross winner Kurt Sametreiter remembered that there was skepticism amongst the troops at first whether Wisch could be a worthy successor of Sepp Dietrich, but he managed to be in every regard.[42] Jupp Steinbüchel served as radio operator in the division's staff company for both Dietrich and Wisch. He later wrote about his impressions of the two officers:

> "Wisch was no Sepp Dietrich, even only judging their nature, since Nordfriesen are heavier types of characters. Sepp Dietrich was a fatherly type with the necessary respect and with exemplary leadership for his men. I believe Wisch, as a commander, gave his best. Between comrades we talked about 'Sepp' one way. When we talked about 'Teddy' in the case of Wisch, it was a little bit different. I can only say that when we drove to the fighting units, Wisch was always very well informed, he always knew what was going on. It happened frequently, that we drove alongside a particular unit commander during an attack which was just developing. The longer the war lasted, the more Teddy Wisch was admired by us, we missed him a lot. Dietrich addressed everyone with an informal YOU, while nobody dared to respond to him the same way. Sepp Dietrich was a respect person of comradely fashion, while Wisch was made of a different kind of wood."[43]

With two orders issued and signed by Dietrich as the commander of the I.SS-Panzer-Korps "Leibstandarte Adolf Hitler" on July 4, 1943, Wisch was promoted to SS-Oberführer and officially given command of the "Leibstandarte."[44] The following day saw the start of Operation "Citadel." Wisch led his Division, as part of the 4.Panzer Armee commanded by Generaloberst Hermann Hoth, from Bjelgorod northwards in an effort to meet up with the 9.Armee of Generaloberst Walter Model. Model's units were fighting their way south from Orel. The objective was to cut off a salient that reached 70 km into the German lines and tied up considerable German troops needed to fight off an expected Allied invasion in France that summer.

The enemy had used the previous three months, in which the Division had been in the process of refitting and restructuring, to heavily fortify the salient around the city of Kursk. Multiple defensive lines included numerous minefields, emplaced flamethrowers, anti-tank ditches, other

[39] Awarded the Diamonds to the Knight's Cross on August 6, 1944, Dietrich also won the Gold Party Badge in 1933 and the Luftwaffe Pilot Observer Badge in Gold with Diamonds, as well as numerous Italian and Romanian decorations. Captured by U.S. troops on May 9, 1945, Dietrich was a defendant in the Malmedy incident war crime trial at Dachau. Sentenced to life in prison on July 17, 1946, he was paroled on October. Arrested by German authorities in August 1956 for his involvement in the 1934 Röhm Putsch, Dietrich was sentenced to 18 months and released on February 2, 1959, due to ill health. He then lived a quiet life in Ludwigsburg, being a senior member of HIAG until his death April 21, 1966. Dietrich's leadership skills and personality, in conjunction with a superior staff and element commanders, attained legendary status for the "Leibstandarte." The resulting adulation of him by those under his command, who affectionately honored him as the "Father" of the "Leibstandarte," rightfully acknowledge him as among the more significant personalities in the history of the Waffen-SS. See photo section and footnote 6.

[40] Email from Erhard Gührs, September 2009. Courtesy of Mike Smeets.

[41] Personal interview with Otto Kumm held at his home in the summer of 2002.

[42] Kurt Sametreiter, Interview conducted by Peter Buchner in June 2010. Sametreiter earned the Knight's Cross on July 31, 1943, as an Oberscharführer with the 3.(schw.)/SS-Panzerjägerabteilung 1 "LSSAH."

[43] Letters to the author from Herrn Steinbüchel dated September 28, 2009, and April 25, 2010.

[44] "Sonderbefehl" dated July 4, 1943, signed by SS-Obergruppenführer Dietrich, see illustration.

dug in tank positions, a well camouflaged bunker system, mortar positions, and additional heavy artillery support.

Sturmmann Günther Borchers was a combat engineer of the 19.Kompanie in Wisch's former SS-Panzer-Grenadier-Regiment 2. He remembered the intensive battles during July as follows:

> "The first Russian positions are in our hand. Here a vehicle drives on a mine and explodes; there a Russian Anti-Tank gun shoots up another one. Our casualties are not as high as we had thought. Now we have to take away every meter of terrain from the Russian in fierce fighting. He fights determinedly in his position and does not want to get captured. We receive fire from the sides and from behind. Numerous planes are in the air and engage into ground combat. The first anti-tank ditch is taken and blown up so our tanks can engage. There isn't fifty meters of unfortified terrain. Everywhere are bunkers, dug in tanks, a minefield, etc. The Russians come with large numbers of tanks, at times as many as 200. Our tanks eliminate lots of them but the Russians always return with more. Where do these come from? We reach the Rollbahn 'Kursk-Bjelgorod.' The battle has not decreased in intensity. Two T-34s penetrate our position and a rocket launcher unit shoots it's weapons. Without paying much attention the T34s advance and fire into the medical assembly position and an ambulance, then they are stopped by a light infantry gun crewman with an anti-tank charge. Both tanks burn immediately."[45]

After six days of powerful advances towards the town of Prochorowka, the Division ground to a painful halt when it clashed with a massive defense line of ditches, anti-tank gun positions, and enemy artillery southeast of the town. Unprotected on its flanks due to the slower advances of the "Totenkopf" and "Das Reich" Divisions, the "Leibstandarte" also had to fight off attacks against its flanks. A new attempt the next day to take Prochorowka led to the largest tank battle in history. But despite the tremendous number of enemy tanks knocked out on that and the following day, the sheer quantity of the Soviet armor thrown into combat did not allow the "Leibstandarte" a favorable outcome of operation "Citadel." Sepp Dietrich described Wisch's personal actions during those days of the operation:

> "During operation 'Citadel' SS-Brigadeführer Wisch, as commander of the 1.SS-Panzer-Grenadier-Division 'LSSAH,' again proved himself as a soldierly leader with high military capabilities as well as strong energy and toughness. With constant personal commitment, he led from the front lines in these hard offensive and defensive battles. The success during the attacks is due to his personal intervention. The armored personnel carrier of the divisional commander within the tank attacks, among the attacking grenadiers, or he rushing from command post to command post straight across the battlefield was a repeatedly seen image during the days of combat. His essential evaluation of all situations, of the strength of his own offensive battles, and his constant presence on the battlefield resulted in the successful defense against enemy attacks by two tank corps on July 12, 1943. The operative defense was also carried out by the SS-Panzer Regiment 1 and the Assault Gun Detachment. Within two hours 130 enemy tanks were destroyed by tanks, assault guns, and close combat troops."[46]

The "Leibstandarte" was pulled out of combat during the following days and ordered to prepare for train transport to an unknown destination. At Dietrich's request, Wisch and his First General Staff Officer (Ia), Sturmbannführer Rudolf Lehmann, flew from Stalino to Berlin on board a HE-111 on July 30, 1943. During a meeting at the Reichs Chancellery the same day, both men were informed that the Division was to be moved immediately by express transport to Northern Italy.

After the American invasion of Sicily on July 10, 1943, the German-Italian alliance threatened to break apart. In the weeks to come, Wisch and the "Leibstandarte" secured vitally important transport routes for the troops engaged in fighting off the invasion in Sicily between the Brenner Pass and Verona, in northern Italy. When rumors about a peace treaty between Italy and the United States emerged, Wisch led his men in operations to disarm the former axis troops in the Po plain, preventing a more serious escalation of hostilities in Italy against German forces.

[45] Personal diary of SS-Untersturmführer Günther Borchers, SS-Panzer-Regiment 1. Original in collection of the author.

[46] "Vorschlagsliste für die Verleihung des Eichenlaubs," dated February 8, 1944, and signed SS-Obergruppenführer und Panzergeneral der Waffen-SS Dietrich. Generalkommando I.SS-Panzerkorps "Leibstandarte SS Adolf Hitler."

Sturmmann Harry Wulf was a member of the Division's 3./Aufklärungsabteilung. He remembered the following during a meeting with the author:

> "During the weeks in Italy we frequently saw our commander 'Teddy' Wisch personally supervising the operations to disarm our former Italian allies. One day, when I proudly brought in two Italian officers I had captured, he had his driver drive up to me, parked the staff car alongside the road and personally congratulated me to my catch!"[47]

On October 30, 1943, while the division was being transported via the Brenner Pass to the St. Pölten area, a surprising order reached Wisch and Lehmann at their command post in Vienna. The Division, renamed the 1.SS-Panzer-Division "Leibstandarte" days earlier, was to deploy immediately to the Western Ukraine. Soviet units during the second half of the year had pushed back German forces more than 350 kilometers and achieved the building of three bridgeheads over the Dnjepr River, passing Kiev and advancing towards Shitomir. The northern wing of Army Group "South" was threatened by encirclement and annihilation, necessitating the intervention of the "Leibstandarte." The Division was rushed into combat and arrived at its operational area at the start of November 1943. Due to the urgency of the deployment there was no time to properly assemble. Some elements were forced to immediately engage in combat upon arrival. Obergruppenführer Dietrich described the following battles under Wisch's leadership as follows:

> "After the disarmament of the troops in all of northern Italy, SS-Brigadeführer Wisch and his Division (since November 1, 1943) were constantly in large battles within the area around Shitomir, Korosten, Bertischew, and southwest of Pogrbischtsche. In every one of the five large operations executed in this area, as well as the defensive battles east of Shitomir and Bertischew and southwest of Bertischew, SS-Brigadeführer Wisch, repeatedly was the soul of the fight due to his personal constant commitment.
>
> During the assault into the enemy's deep flank from Korin, over Ssolowjewka to Katscherowo at the road Shitomir-Kiew from November 14 – 18, 1943, strong enemy forces had cut off the transport road. After the breakthrough of the armored group had settled down near Swolewjewka, the enemy in Brussiloff tried to stop the advance of the Division through counterattacks. Through an offensive flank cover by parts of the SS-Panzer-Grenadier-Regiment 2 and the reconnaissance detachment, the Division managed to secure the ground gained towards the east.
>
> During an enemy breakthrough in the west on November 16, 1943, SS-Brigadeführer Wisch, who had just returned from a reconnaissance, dispatched several assault guns and parts of the armored III./ SS-Panzer-Grenadier-Regiment 2 and destroyed an enemy group in battalion strength with a dashing counterattack he personally led. That hindered the intended taking of the road.
>
> After this breakthrough towards the transport road, the Division was assigned to destroy several strong enemy infantry groups infiltrating through the woods east of Radomischl. Without awaiting the assembly of the Division due to the extremely bad road conditions, SS-Brigadeführer Wisch put all combat ready assault guns with mounted infantry into action. With them and an additional armored battle group operating in the northeast, he quickly gained ground. In a few days the battle groups were united in the rear of the opponent and a pocket was built with the engagement of the remaining elements of the Division that destroyed the enemy.
>
> Since December 5, 1943, the Division fought in the area east of Tschernjachoff. It was assigned to establish contact between the XIII.Armeekorps and the LIX.Armeekorps east of Korosten. This was accomplished by destroying the enemy troops in the area of Radomischl. SS-Brigadeführer initiated this operation with a 30 kilometers wide assault into the rear of the enemy in front of the XIII.Armeekorps with a strong armored group. Without regard for heavy fighting developing in the rear and flank of the divisions of the XIII.Armeekorps, an additional daring assault by SS-Brigadeführer Wisch destroyed the enemy bridgehead near Radomischl.
>
> The success of this undertaking, for which the Commander in Chief of the 4.Panzer Armee, General Raus, personally expressed his recognition during his presence in the division command post, was due to the boldness, bravery, and almost superhuman efforts of the tank crews and grenadiers. The success must also to a large scale be thanked to SS-Brigadeführer Wisch, who on a daily basis led his troops from the front lines.

[47] Interview with Harry Wulf at his home in Horneburg in the summer of 2001.

On December 20, 1943, the Division received orders to move east with the 1. and 7.Panzer Divisions from the area east of Korosten to repel and destroy the enemy. Due to the tangled, swampy, and bushy landscape, the attack spearheads of the divisions went out of their original attack routes after throwing the enemy out of his field positions. Before more confusion occurred, SS-Brigadeführer Wisch personally assumed command of his forward grenadiers and tanks with a compass in his hand. Since the leadership of the battle groups from the command post was almost impossible due to the constantly cut-off communication ways in that partisan area, Wisch remained in the front lines during all day and night attacks. During the time of the defensive battles, against most of the 3.Guards Tank Army, Wisch proved his leadership skills and personal bravery.

Despite the unfavorable tank situation caused by the long march from Korosten to the area east of Shitomir, Wisch managed to hold up the massive enemy tank attacks considerably. He did this with a concentration of tanks on the focal points and additionally destroyed enemy tank forces by creating anti-tank fronts using tanks that were being repaired. These tough battles east and southwest of Bertischew saw recognition for the Division in the Wehrmacht Daily Report of December 31, 1943, and in a personal teletype sent by Generalfeldmarschall von Manstein on January 13, 1944."[48]

The Wehrmacht Daily Report of December 31, 1943, read:

"During the heavy defensive battles in the area around Shitomir, the 1.SS-Panzer-Division under leadership of Oberführer Wisch distinguished itself with exemplary battle sprit."

Sepp Dietrich noted the successes under Wisch's command during the Russian campaign battles of July 5-12, 1943, and from November 6, 1943, to January 31, 1944. In those battles the "Leibstandarte" destroyed or captured:

1,124 T34 tanks
12 KW tanks
5 armored scout cars
89 other small tanks
(6) 7.62 guns
34 guns 12.2mm
5 anti-aircraft guns
7 automatic guns
97 other guns
227 medium anti-tank guns (3.7mm to 4.5mm)
1,056 heavy anti-tank guns (7.62m)
12 grenade launchers (50mm)
45 grenade launchers (82mm)
73 grenade launchers (122mm)
533 anti-tank rifles
638 machine guns
575 machine pistols
2,003 Rifles
9 emplaced flamethrower barriers
37 aircraft
334 other vehicles
98 horse drawn vehicles
2,933 prisoners
16,541 enemy killed

Dietrich further commented on the personal accomplishments of Wisch more significantly for that period. The battles compelled him to request an award for the "Leibstandarte" commander:

"I consider SS-Brigadeführer Wisch, because of his constantly proven bravery, his never-ending highest proof of worth and the excellent leadership of his Division, worthy of the award of the Oakleaves to the Knight's Cross of the Iron Cross and request permission to present SS-Brigadeführer Wisch with this award."[49]

Jupp Steinbüchel, an Oberscharführer in the 2./Nachrichtenabteilung, recalled Wisch's constant acts of bravery and high personal commitment during the difficult weeks of fighting near Shitomir. In his personal diary that was shared with the author, he recalled the first days of

[48] "Vorschlagsliste für die Verleihung des Eichenlaubs," dated February 8, 1944, and signed SS-Obergruppenführer und Panzergeneral der Waffen-SS Dietrich. Generalkommando I.SS-Panzerkorps "Leibstandarte SS Adolf Hitler."

[49] "Vorschlagsliste für die Verleihung des Eichenlaubs," dated February 8, 1944, signed SS-Obergruppenführer und Panzergeneral der Waffen-SS Dietrich. Generalkommando I.SS-Panzerkorps "Leibstandarte SS Adolf Hitler." In the Oakleaves recommendation Dietrich refers to Wisch at the rank he held when the proposal was written, the events having occurred when he was an Oberführer. The proposal included the enemy material destroyed or captured listed.

December 1943 when he served as the radio operator in Wisch's scout car:

> "The following days I am given an extra task. Commander Wisch needs a radio operator for his armored scout car and that function I will take over now. Now every morning we drive out to the front with the Oberführer. The roads are hopelessly muddy, but the scout car takes us everywhere. Many times we are glad that we are armored, because the commander likes it rough! Almost every day he accompanies one attack. One time with Peiper, the next time with Kraas or Kuhlmann, depending on what the situation demands. On my birthday we drive a dashing attack with Peiper. The Russians take considerable losses in men and material."[50]

Steinbüchel also shared a somewhat amusing anecdote of an occurrence that took place in the winter of 1943. He wrote the author the following:

> "In December 1943 we were at a command post, I forgot the exact unit. Wisch and his Ia, Rudolf Lehmann, were sitting on a slope with their legs spread out and they were talking to each other. Suddenly an unexploded enemy tank round zoomed over to us and penetrated into the ground between Wisch's legs. Surprised, Wisch poked into the hole with a piece of wood and said: 'For once we had some luck!' But there was no special attention caused by this and soon we drove back to our command post."[51]

Oberscharführer Kurt Sametreiter remembered the following story: In early 1944 a women's theater group had visited the division to entertain the troops. Sametreiter and his men, who had already had one or two drinks, got so bored with the performance these women were giving, that he and four of his men instinctively got up from their seats and sneaked into the backstage area of the theater. Moments later the five soldiers appeared up on stage wearing women's dresses, giving their own performance and dancing wildly! Obersturmbannführer Joachim Peiper was not at all been amused by Sametreiter's conduct and had him report to the divisional commander, Brigadeführer Wisch. Peiper explained, in Wisch's presence, that it was totally unprofessional for Sametreiter, an NCO and Knight's Cross winner to mingle in such a way with the men under his command. Sametreiter, however, defended his conduct explaining that for him it was absolutely normal to mix with his men the way he did the night before, because it was obviously not a problem for his superiors that he would have to mingle with his men when they were fighting and laying in the mud together. Much to the surprise to everyone present at the hearing, including Obersturmbannführer Peiper, Wisch spontaneously agreed to Sametreiter's view of the situation, but ordered him to not wear women's dresses the next time they went into battle against the enemy.

On February 16, 1944, the Supreme Commander of the Armed Forces announced the 393rd award of the Oakleaves to Theodor Wisch, commander of the 1.SS-Panzer-Division "Leibstandarte." Only two weeks before, at the age of 36, Wisch had been promoted to SS-Brigadeführer und Generalmajor der Waffen-SS. In his formal request Obergruppenführer Sepp Dietrich wrote about the Division commander:

> "Wisch is a straight and, impressive personality. During all missions he's exemplary brave. His performance as commander of the 1.SS-Panzer Division 'Leibstandarte SS Adolf Hitler' was especially emphasized in the Armed Forces Daily Report. Wisch is an exemplary SS leader and very well suited to be divisional commander."

On February 26, 1944, a message of the Wehrmachts Adjutantur of the Führer arrived at the divisional command post, requesting Wisch to personally report to Hitler's headquarters to be presented with his Oakleaves to the Knight's Cross. Together with Obergruppenführer Dietrich, Oberführer Fritz Witt, and Obersturmbannführer Max Wünsche, Wisch traveled to the Obersalzberg.[52] There the men

[50] Personal postwar written war diary "2.Kompanie – N.A.1," written by Herrn Jupp Steinbüchel.

[51] Letter from Herrn Steinbüchel to the author dated September 28, 2009.

(Footnote 52 see page 20)

were initially received by Obersturmführer Otto Günsche, Hitler's personal adjutant. Later, in a short ceremony Wisch received the Oakleaves personally from Hitler.

Having become ill during his stay at Berchtesgaden to receive his award, Wisch had to undergo medical treatment and was only able to return to the Division at the end of March 1944. His duties were temporarily taken over by the divisional Ia, Obersturmbannführer Rudolf Lehmann. SS war correspondent Kurbjuhn accompanied the Division, writing about the unit and Wisch's difficult leadership task under extremely adverse combat conditions in 1944:

> "Since November it is never quiet and during the past months the Division has lived through the most difficult campaign in its history. Frequently mentioned in the Armed Forces Daily Report, today the Division is fighting in the area near Tarnopol against a superior enemy in the ice and mud of the Rollbahn. The number of its troops has melted down. Many of the fallen were known to the division commander by name. He frequently knew the exact circumstances of their lives and one or another had been a close comrade to him. The difficult farewell of his fallen soldiers does not make his task easier. It seems that he never wants to think of the glory of his Division, in which he participated. He sees long lines of quiet shapes, which are buried along the long roads of this war and march behind the old 'Leibstandarte' as it moves towards new assignments."[53]

After further continuous combat, the "Leibstandarte" was finally pulled from the frontline in mid-April 1944 and sent by train for refit to the Turnhout area of northern Belgium. Wisch, exhausted by the enormous amounts of physical and mental stress of the past months, entered treatment for a heart problem at the SS hospital in Bad Nauheim on April 26, 1944. Following his recovery, he returned to the Division on May 25, 1944.[54] Obersturmbannführer Rudolf Lehmann (Ia) oversaw the activities of the division during Wisch's absence until he as well became seriously ill and passed the duties of General Staff Officer on to Obersturmbannführer Erich Grensing.[55]

On June 6, 1944, the long expected Allied invasion into Northern France took place. Supported by more than 5,000 ships and 11,000 aircraft, the American and Commonwealth armed forces landed on the beaches of Normandy. After having spent several days on alert at the Pas de Calais, the "Leibstandarte" was finally mobilized on June 17th. Moving mostly at night to an area south of Caen, the Division was under endless aerial attacks. A month later, alongside its sister division the 12.SS-Panzer-Division "Hitlerjugend," it engaged in numerous defensive battles against Allied troops around Caen and later Falaise. In the summer of 1944 a war correspondent wrote about Wisch's leadership of the Division in some of its most desperate battles:

> "In his vicinity all theoretical discussions rapidly suffer breathing difficulties. From his quiet self confidence the certainty shines out, that the lives of men at war have very simple words and the big words might only make an impression in the nervous home country. But not at all where tanks and assault guns rule the hour. 'Because the one who always has faith does not need to be taught or told,' he says in the cool way of a 'Schleswig-Holsteiner' when he starts to talk about his men at the invasion front

[52] Max Wünsche (SS# 153 508) was born on April 20, 1914, in Kittlitz and joined the SS in July 1933. Graduating with the 2nd class at Junkerschule Bad Tölz, he was commissioned on April 20, 1936. He then served as a platoon leader with the 9. and 17.Kompanien of the "Leibstandarte." Promoted to Obersturmführer on September 11, 1938, Wünsche served as an ordnance officer to Adolf Hitler in the "Führer Begleitkommando" from October 1938 until the Western Campaign, where he led a platoon in the 15./Kradschützenkompanie. Promoted to Hauptsturmführer on May 25, 1940, from June to December he returned to service with Hitler before becoming Adjutant (IIa) of the "Leibstandarte." Wünsche was given command of the Sturmgeschütz Battalion on February 15, 1942, and after taking a three month General Staff course in Berlin was promoted to Sturmbannführer on September 1, 1942. On October 22, 1942, he was given command of the I./Panzer-Regiment 1. There he won the German Cross in Gold on February 25, 1943, and the Knight's Cross three days later. With the creation of the I.SS-Panzer-Korps, Wünsche was given command of SS-Panzer-Regiment 12 of the 12.SS-Panzer-Division "Hitlerjugend." Promoted to Obersturmbannführer on January 30, 1944, he won the Oakleaves to the Knight's Cross on August 11, 1944, following a recommendation by Kurt Meyer. After escaping the Falaise pocket he was captured by Canadian forces on August 24, 1944. Max Wünsche returned to Germany four years later and passed away in Munich on April 17, 1995.

[53] Report written by SS-Kriegsberichter (War correspondent) Kurbjuhn, used in a leaflet handed out to family members and veterans at Theodor Wisch's funeral in 1995.

[54] Soldbuch of Theodor Wisch, page 12-13, Krankheit entry code -49- (= Heart disease), according to the "Fehlertabelle für die Deutsche Wehrmacht," Bundesversorgungsgesetz volume V, A20 ff.

[55] Erich Grensing was born August 18, 1910, in Alt Stelitz and graduated with the 1935 class of Junkerschule Braunschweig. In 1939 Grensing served as staff Ic with the SS-V.T.-Division (mot) that later became "Das Reich." Promoted to Obersturmbannführer on November 9, 1943, he assumed the post as Ia of the "Leibstandarte" in late May 1944. Severely wounded in late August 1944 by enemy artillery fire, he was replaced by the Division's Ic and later O1, Hauptsturmführer Hans Bernhard. During his recovery Grensing was formally assigned to the SS-Führungshauptamt leadership reserve on October 16, 1944.

during a pause in the fighting. It was an interview that was often interrupted, the 'pause' being filled with never-ending attacks by the enemy fighter-bombers. They were circling above the woods in which the command post was located. In these words the pride sounded through of the invulnerability his Division lives on."[56]

Brigadeführer Wisch himself recalled the actions of the 1.SS-Panzer-Division under his command during August 1944 years later. In response to questions by the U.S. Army he stated:

"1) At the beginning of August the Division was engaged in hard defensive battles in the area southeast of Caen. The Division was ordered to withdraw swiftly, after relief by an infantry division, to the new combat area northeast of Mortain in preparation for a penetration by assault on Avranches. The relief was delayed by the late arrival of single elements of the infantry division. At first, the SS-Panzer-Division could only partly be set on the march. The Panzer battalion (I.), Panzer-Grenadier battalion (III./2), and engineer battalion marched as advanced units. The date for the march was 6 August 1944.

At the meeting at the Corps (General von Funck) it was ordered that the tanks be deployed immediately after arrival for an attack on St. Barthelemy. For this attack, they were subordinated to the 2.Panzer-Division. Because of road difficulties and technical defects, the tanks came directly out of the fighting, the battalion arrived in the late evening and night, and didn't arrive in the assembly area until the morning hours of August 7, 1944. Due to the lack of infantry and in order to exploit an eventual success in the fighting to further advance, the Panzer-Grenadier-Bataillon that had already arrived was subordinated to the Armored commander. This was the one to capture St. Berthelemy. The discussions with General von Funck were short, I don't remember any more details. Principally, he insisted on the procurement of all units of the Division, regarding which I had no influence initially, because of the difficulties of relief in the previous area.

2) The Division arrived in the new combat area via Falaise, Argentan, Flairs Ger. I don't remember if the main street was used to Tinchebray or whether from Flers via a side street.

3) At the beginning of August, the Division was no longer in the best condition. Heavy combat losses were sustained.

a) Losses in men, especially in the two Panzer-Grenadier Regiments were very high. (I am not in a position to make any other numerical statements). Panzer III, IV and V had on hand about 60 – 65 men who arrived in the new combat area, some in poor shape caused by the march. Up till then the artillery had fewer losses.

b) Alencon was the supply base of the Division. While at first sufficient, supply was made more and more difficult by increasingly hard air attacks (especially fuel and ammunition); finally it was nearly impossible since the supply columns were attacked by air even at night.

4) On the march to the fighting position, the Division was repeatedly attacked, most of the time with single aircraft. The losses through those attacks were less.

5) As ordered by the Corps, the attack was led by the 2.Panzer-Division. When the command was taken over by the 'LAH' the formations advancing along the street from St. Barthelemy to Juvigny were stopped immediately east of Juvigny. They had losses in the Panzers by anti-tank guns and Panzer and some were lost by rockets from aircraft. Now the Division had to gather its forces and bring the attack forward, but it was hindered by commitment by the Corps in a different way to proceed. To protect the advance formation against encirclement, units were needed which were still arriving. There was no connection with the flanks and later on only with the right. Because of the unfavorable terrain, Panzers and trucks had to drive on the secondary streets and lanes. During the daytime their movements were made nearly impossible by enemy air attacks; at night, for lack of escort infantry in sufficient strength, movement was without success.

Meanwhile, the Division had heavy losses in men. It lost nearly 1/3 of its Panzers through air attack but had pushed forward to about 2-3 kilometers east of Juvigny.

6) My opinion is the attack failed for various reasons. The real situation at Avranches seemed to have become known by the higher command very late, or the decision for our own activity was postponed too long. There was a lack of attack

[56] Report written by SS-War correspondent Kurbjuhn, used in a leaflet handed out to family members and veterans at Theodor Wisch´s funeral in 1995.

formations for this push. At first suitable units had to be relieved in other combat areas. Other factors were strong American Air Forces, the complete lack of support from the Luftwaffe, and the unfavorable terrain for Panzer units.

7) There were considerable losses in the Panzers and trucks by rockets of the Typhoons of the RAF. There were fewer losses from American tanks. There were heavy losses in our own infantry from American infantry, especially the infantry which accompanied the Panzers. After the failure of the breakthrough at Avranches, the Division was ordered to assemble for new fighting in the woods north of Alencon. Those units not fit for combat as a signal battalion and units of the artillery not fit as advance guard of the Division were attached shortly after their arrival. After that, the Division got new orders. It was committed for defense in the area of Fromentel with the front to the south and reached the area through Flers, Fromentel. During the night August 18/19, the rest of the Division moved into the area northeast of Argentan coming via Putanges, an American tank unit had pushed through and stopped between the railroad and the streets in the woods south of Fromentel.

Counterattacks by our own Panzers, promising success, were impossible because of fuel shortage. Now the Division was encircled.

8) On August 19, combat groups of the Division in the encirclement were committed by order of the Corps for shielding necessary sectors together with the Panzers. Different parts of the Division had no connection with the others for the most part. Therefore, commands were only possible by individual orders. The break-out of the encirclement was made in the early morning hours of August 20, 1944. After the break-out of the foremost part of the Division at St Lambert, I wanted to be in the march as part of my staff. At that time I was sorely wounded and was able to get out of the encirclement after some attempts over St. Lambert to the northeast."[57]

Jupp Steinbüchel recalled having seen Wisch the last time on August 18th at the bridge near Putanges, heading towards St. Lambert:

"That night there was a radio message from Wisch to the Aufklärungsabteilung: Where can the Division cross? I was then able to dispatch a reply to Wisch from Sturmbannführer Gustav Knittel. The evening of August 20, the leadership staff of the Division rolled through St.Lambert, but without Wisch!"[58]

Hauptsturmführer Hans Bernhard, the Division's Ic, who had temporarily taken over the position of Ia from seriously wounded Obersturmbannführer Erich Grensing, was the only person with Wisch the moment he was wounded. He described the situation to the author as follows:

"During the invasion we were encircled together with other Army units in the Falaise pocket and we managed to escape. Me, Wisch, and three to four other officers were in a small forest. A superior General arrived, gave orders for the current situation. Then Wisch and I walked out of the forest to the east over a beautiful field and I told him: 'Brigadeführer, as a man of the artillery, I would shoot into here!' that was only from my gut instinct, since the area was visually not accessible. But I had that gut feeling. Wisch was the born infantry man and did not at all react to my comment.

Suddenly a single round exploded and Wisch and I fell into the dirt. It was unbelievable! Only one single artillery round, shot directly at us by coincidence! Teddy Wisch was a big man and I was laying beside him on the field, with only a small wound package at hand. And now, what to do? I had nothing and to carry him was impossible. Suddenly an armored personnel carrier drove up to us. Sitting in it was Obersturmbannführer Steineck, the commander of the artillery regiment, whom I knew very well. I stopped him and told him: 'Out, immediately! The Brigadeführer is severely wounded and needs to get in!' The personnel carrier drove down to a small village called 'Dives', where a very old and simple stone bridge crossed a small river. We could not cross with our vehicle. In a giant barn I laid down 'Teddy' Wisch. Since I had been in the artillery trade many years, I placed Wisch so that he would not be harmed by more artillery shelling."

[57] Generalmajor der Waffen-SS Theodor Wisch, Responses to questions regarding 1.SS-Panzer-Division in August 1944, National Archives Manuscript B-358, RG 338, College Park, MD, U.S.A.

[58] Letter from Herrn Jupp Steinbüchel to the author dated April 25, 2010.

Hauptsturmführer Bernhard then got another armored vehicle from an Army unit operating in the area on the other side of the bridge, which had not been in proper condition to cross with the first armored halftrack. They were able to continue Wisch's evacuation. The Division commander was lifted on board and laid in the back. The evacuation continued slowly, since the roads were heavily congested with destroyed and fleeing vehicles as well as personnel trying to escape encirclement by the Allied units. Bernhard ran alongside and in front of the transport, trying to clear the way for them. But when further advance was almost impossible he ordered the transport to drive off the road, down a small slope, and then continuing alongside a small river. Suddenly the armored transport was hit and crawled to a complete standstill. It had been hit by an enemy anti-tank round and the driver was killed instantly. Bernhard, who had been running alongside the vehicle, was stunned. He checked the Brigadeführer's condition and was relieved to see him alive and fully conscious. Once more the four-leaf clover Wisch used to carry with him in his Soldbuch brought him good luck.[59]

Bernhard wasted no time and ran back on foot to the German lines, and was able to locate an Army unit which immediately provided Bernhard with a vehicle and a driver. Together they rushed back and rescued Wisch from the wreckage, loading him onto the other transport for further evacuation.[60]

Due to his quick reaction and efforts, Hauptsturmführer Bernhard secured Brigadeführer Wisch's timely evacuation from the Falaise pocket through a narrow corridor desperately held open by the various German units, including SS-Regiment 4 "Der Führer," under the command of Obersturmbannführer and later swords winner Otto Weidinger. Wisch was one of three Generals, 300 officers, and more than 4,000 men escaping capture or complete annihilation by the Allied forces at the Falaise pocket.[61]

Severely wounded on his right leg, Wisch needed intensive medical attention.[62] After initial provisional treatment at the front, he was transferred to the "Chirurgisches Sonderlazarett des O.K.H." (Special Surgeon Hospital of the Supreme Command of the Army) on August 23rd. He finally entered the SS Hospital at Hohenlychen, 80 kilometers north of Berlin, on August 30, 1944.[63] One day earlier, on August 29, 1944, Oberstgruppenführer und Generaloberst der Waffen-SS Dietrich sent a telegram addressed to Hauptsturmführer Otto Günsche, Adjutant to the Führer:

> "I recommend SS-Brigadeführer Wisch, Kommandeur 1.SS Panzer Division "Leibstandarte" for the Oakleaves with Swords. During the battles between Caen and Falaise, Wisch and his Division performed outstandingly. In a never-ending effort Wisch halted all breakthrough attempts. A severe break-in on the left flank was finished off with a dashing counter-attack, carried out on his initiative. Also in the encirclement area the Division held its position against the heaviest enemy attacks, repeatedly counterattacked by its commander. The day of the outbreak Wisch led his infantry personally, rallying them forward through never before experienced enemy fire on the very narrow escape route. Theodor Wisch was seriously wounded fighting on front line. Wisch is especially worthy of the highest award due to his spirited composure and successful leadership."[64]

---

[59] The four-leaf clover survived the war and is still part of Wisch's Soldbuch today.

[60] Phone conversation with Hans Bernhard on August 22, 2009, and September 6, 2009. Wisch's own report on the circumstances of his escape from the pocket of Falaise in Tiemann's "Die Leibstandarte," Volume IV/1, 1986, are not completely accurate, in virtue of the various long telephone conversations with former SS-Hauptsturmführer Bernhard explaining every aspect of the situation. Bernhard was the only person together with Wisch during the crucial moments. There was no meeting called in with the regimental commanders of the division, and Wisch was not accompanied by his Division-Adjutant SS-Sturmbannführer Beutler, but rather his Ic, Bernhard. The author assumes that Wisch had no detailed and complete recollection about the situation anymore and did confuse the names of his adjutants/ General staff officers and the circumstances before the explosion of the grenade near him when he sent the report to Mr. Tiemann for the book series after the war.

[61] See Mr. Mark C. Yerger's authorized biography on SS-Obersturmbannführer Otto Weidinger, published by Schiffer Military Publishing, 2000.

[62] "Zur Person," Interrogation protocol, LKPA Niedersachsen, Sonderkommission Z, Friedrichsgabe dated December 1, 1964, Bundesarchiv, Signatur B 162/3145. Wisch was not wounded on both legs, as frequently mentioned in other biographies. Former SS-Hauptsturmführer Bernhard, who was with Wisch when he was wounded, explained the author in a phone conversation on October 18, 2009, that he remembered the grenade exploding 15-20 meters behind them to the right, which supports the fact that Wisch was only wounded on the right leg and not on both of his legs.

[63] Personalakte Theodor Wisch and Soldbuch, issued July 11, 1943, page 12. Wisch was not awarded the Golden Wound Badge as sometimes mentioned in other biographies, even though his suffered wound would have clearly qualified him for this award. There are no confirmations in his SS-Personalakte, personal Soldbuch, nor does an award certificate exist.

[64] Personalakte Theodor Wisch.

On August 30, 1944, Adolf Hitler awarded Theodor Wisch the 94th Swords of the Knight's Cross of the German Wehrmacht. The same day Brigadeführer Wilhelm Mohnke arrived at the Division's staff quarters and officially took over command of the unit.[65] In the days before that command of the Division had been temporarily assumed by the commander of Panzer-Artillerie-Regiment 1, Obersturmbannführer Franz Steineck, with Hauptsturmführer Bernhard acting as Ia.[66]

Waldemar Heinrich, a former Oberscharführer in the Leibstandarte, was Theodor Wisch's half-.brother. He told the author how he met Wisch for the first time in his life at the SS Hospital at Hohenlychen:

> "He was in his bed, the room had a double door. I arrived on time, but had to wait since it was still resting time after lunch. Later I knocked on the door and reported very correctly. Then he said 'Come here and get yourself a chair. Do you smoke?' He did not smoke at all and only occasionally had a cup of wine. He was very modest. He gave me a pack of cigarettes and we talked for almost an hour. Naturally it was a strange sensation at first, since I saw him as a Brigadeführer and a superior officer, but that was quickly forgotten after we had exchanged our first words."[67]

Theodor Wisch was formally assigned to the SS-Führungshauptamt (SS-Leadership Main Office) on November 9, 1944.[68] He and his wife had their fourth child, Henning Wisch, on January 30, 1945. In April sad news reached him, learning that his second brother, Oberscharführer Hans Wisch, was killed near Nürnberg on April 24, 1945.[69]

Wisch's severe wounds did not allow him to return to the Division he had served with for eleven years.[70] In early January 1945 Himmler proposed Wisch for a seat in the Reichstag, replacing Brigadeführer Kurt Hintze, who had been killed in a bombing raid. The end of the war in May prevented Wisch from ever assuming that new responsibility.[71]

Taken prisoner by the British at his home in Heide/Holstein, Wisch was transferred to a POW hospital in Swindon/Wills, United Kingdom. In October 1947 he was moved to Neuengamme POW camp near Hamburg,

---

[65] According to former Hauptsturmführer Hans Bernhard, a division staff was practically non-existent. He continued acting as Brigadeführer Mohnke's Ia until SS-Sturmbannführer Ziemssen took over the position in September 1944. Bernhard then became the division's O1.

[66] Franz Szcezeponek (SS# 42 508) was born on March 23, 1909, in Hindenburg, and in 1942 changed his name to Steineck. He joined the Allgemeine-SS on August 1, 1931, with the 1./III./23. SS Standarte in Oppeln. In mid-March 1933 Steineck moved to the 13./Leibstandarte as one of the initial 117 and became an Oberscharführer on March 10, 1935. Commissioned on November 9, 1936, he acted as a platoon leader with the 13.Kompanie, and from June 12, 1939, as Kompanie Chef. After leading his unit in Poland he was promoted to Hauptsturmführer on December 1, 1939. Steineck transferred to the 16.Kompanie in January 1940 and won the Iron Cross 1st Class on June 7, 1940. He then led the V.Bataillon from August 1940 and was promoted to Sturmbannführer at the start of that September. On January 6, 1942, Steineck moved to the Artillerie Regiment and took command of the I.Abteilung in late April, as well as being deputy commander. Promoted to Obersturmbannführer on November 9, 1943, he simultaneously commanded SS-Artillerie Abteilung 101 (I.SS-Panzer-Korps) at the start of the Normandy campaign. Steineck assumed temporary command of the Division for ten days after Theodor Wisch was wounded at Falaise. He next succeeded Gustav Mertsch as commander of the Artillerie Regiment on September 1, 1944, and was awarded the German Cross in Gold for his Abteilung and Regiment commands on December 30, 1944, from a recommendation by Walter Staudinger. Steineck continued to officially lead the Regiment until the end of the war. However, it was the divisional O1, Hauptsturmführer Hans Bernhard, who commanded the unit on a daily basis during the final weeks of fighting in Hungary and Austria. Franz Steineck survived the war and died in Neumarkt on December 24, 1971.

[67] Interview with Waldemar Heinrich at his home in Hasloh on June 17, 2001.

[68] Deutsche Dienststelle (WaSt) V/25-677/173 (1), dated July 1, 2004.

[69] Information Volksbund Deutsche Kriegsgräberstiftung. Hans J. Wisch is buried at the Kriegsgräberstätte Hofkirchen (Germany), Row 30, Lot 8.

[70] Contrary to previous accounts, Wisch´s legs were not amputated during or after the war. His hip remained a permanent health problem, and he had to use a walking stick according to later postwar photos and an interview with his stepbrother, Waldemar Heinrich.

[71] Personalakte Theodor Wisch, Letter to Reichsführer-SS Persönlicher Stab dated January 25, 1945. "Namenhaftmachung eines SS-Führers für die Neubesetzung des Reichstagssitzes des durch den Bombenterror gefallenen SS-Brigadeführer Hintze." Signed SS-Standartenführer R.Brandt.

Germany.[72] After five months of standing trial in front of a Spruchgericht in Bergedorf/Hamburg, the court ruled in favor of Theodor Wisch, dropping all charges brought against him.[73] A revision of the case requested by the state attorney was later rejected:

> "The defendant entered voluntarily into the Allgemeine-SS in November 1930 and in March 1933 the SS-Verfügungstruppe, later the Waffen-SS. He stayed with this formation until the end of the war, finally acting as a Divisional commander with the rank of SS-Brigadeführer. During the war, with the exception of the time between January 1940 and June 1941, where he was commander of the Wach-Battalion of the Leibstandarte in Berlin-Lichterfelde, he had multiple stays in hospitals as a consequence of wounds received during front duty. He is the recipient of high war decorations including the Knight's Cross with Oakleaves and Swords. The court has exonerated the defendant in regards to the actions of the SS for the abuse and murder of prisoners of war, the forced labor work program, the persecution of Jews, acts committed in the occupied territories, and the persecution of political prisoners.
>
> It believes the defendant to be of good character, honest, and a sincere person who is only interested in his military career and its associated narrow focus on soldiering. Therefore and in virtue of his denial and missing further evidence, the court is dismissing all charges against the defendant."[74]

As with many of his former comrades, Wisch had a difficult time integrating himself as a civilian into post-war Germany. Even after receiving medical treatment in various military POW hospitals until 1948, he had to continue seeing civilian doctors until 1950 before being able to think about the beginning of a new career.[75] Based on his pre-war degree in agriculture, he finally managed to work for the "Verband Rotbunte Schleswig-Holsteiner e.V. Neumünster" / "Red Holstein Cattle Breeder Association e.V. Neumünster" in his home state of Schleswig-Holstein. There, according to his stepbrother, he knew everything and everyone.[76]

On September 15, 1957, Theodor Wisch unsuccessfully ran as a candidate for the "Deutsche Reichspartei" (Landesliste Schleswig Holstein) at the third parliamentary elections of the German Federal Republic.[77] He joined the Waffen-SS veteran's association HIAG and participated in many of their meetings, including the early "Nordmark-Treffen" in October 1963 and 1964 in Rendsburg.

Despite being exonerated in his early postwar trial that confirmed him as a career military officer, Wisch suffered personally from recurring trials or investigations of others. In December 1964, nearly two decades after all potential personal charges against him were dismissed, an investigation began in Niedersachsen into the conduct of several former members of the I./SS-Panzer-Grenadier-Regiment 2 and their involvement in the killing of 16 Greek and Italian Jewish refugees at a hotel in Meina, near the Lago Maggiore, on September 16, 1943.

Despite the unauthorized actions of those involved in concert with the SD, Wisch endured the personal humiliation of a career military officer being interrogated about the event due to being in command of the "Leibstandarte" at the time. Even though no accusations or formal charges were made against him personally, he suffered from social repercussions of the investigation due to his connection to the "Leibstandarte" and the general public's postwar sentiment with regard to the Waffen-SS in Germany.

[72] Interrogation protocol, LKPA Niedersachsen, Sonderkommission Z, Friedrichsgabe dated December 1, 1964, and Neumünster dated December 3, 1964. Bundesarchiv Signatur B 162/3145. According to information from the Deutsche Dienststelle, WaSt, dated July 01, 2004 (V/25-667/173 (1), Wisch was taken prisoner by the British on May 18, 1945, and transferred to Neuengamme POW camp near Hamburg, Germany, on October 10, 1947.

[73] Spruchgericht, 13. Spruchkammer, AZ: 9 Sp.Ls. 136/48 – 13/37; Spruchgerichtsverfahren gegen den SS-Brigadeführer und Generalmajor der Waffen-SS Theodor Wisch, Sitzung vom 08.03.1948.

[74] "Revision der Anklagebehörde gegen das Urteil der 13.Spruchkammer des Spruchgerichts Bergedorf am 8. März 1948." Geschäftsnummer: 2Sp. Ss.2123/48, 9Sp. Ls 136/48 (Bergedorf).

[75] Interrogation protocol, LKPA Niedersachsen, Sonderkommission Z, Friedrichsgabe dated December 1, 1964. Bundesarchiv Signatur B 162/3145.

[76] "Der Freiwillige" 41. Jahrgang, Heft 3, March 1995. "Nachruf" written by Hubert Meyer.

[77] "M.d.B. Volksvertretung im Wiederaufbau 1946-1961. Bundestagskandidaten und Mitglieder der westzonalen Vorparlamente. Eine biographische Dokumentation," Martin Schumacher, Droste Verlag, Düsseldorf 2000. Information courtesy of Herrn Andreas Schulz, Berlin.

Wisch became an honorary member of the "Truppenkameradschaft 1.Panzer-Korps" veteran's group on September 1, 1969, and was an honorary member of the "Truppenkameradschaft der 1.Kompanie "LAH," together with former comrades Heinrich Springer, Albert Stenwedel, Otto Günsche, Martin Gross, Willy Stratmann, and many others. He received the association's first honor ring at a reunion in 1981.[78]

Besides spending many vacations with his children, he often visited his stepbrother at his nearby home north of Hamburg. Both used to eat green eel, Wisch's favorite dish, and talked about various aspects of life, rather than about their war experiences.

"A good and calm character, he was. Very popular. That's why they used to call him Teddy Wisch," his stepbrother Waldemar Heinrich told the author during a meeting at his home in late 2002. Theodor Wisch celebrated his 85th birthday with his family and former comrades and Knight's Cross holders Heinrich Springer, Albert Stenwedel, and Ernst Barkmann at the home of one of his sons.

After being ill for many months, Theodor Wisch passed away at the Pinneberg district hospital on January 11, 1995.[79] A ceremony in which former Obersturmbannführer Hubert Meyer spoke the eulogy was held for Theodor Wisch on January 19, 1995, at the Hamburg-Öjendorf cemetery.[80] Apart from family members and friends, former "Leibstandarte" commander Wilhelm Mohnke and Otto Günsche attended. Today Theodor Wisch rests in a cemetery east of Hamburg.

[78] Verleihungsliste "Ehrenringe der Truppenkameradschaft der 1.Kompanie." Estate of Willy Stratmann, First speaker "Truppenkameradschaft 1.Kompanie." Archive of the author.

[79] Wisch's death was registered at the Standesamt Pinneberg on January 16, 1995, under internal reference number 36/1995.

[80] The original newspaper add mentioned January 26, 1995, at 3 PM, but the date was later changed.

BIBLIOGRAPHY

Private Collections
Mark C. Yerger archives
Thomas Fischer archives
Author's archive

Archives and Institutions
Bundesarchiv, Freiburg (Militärarchiv), Koblenz and Ludwigsburg, Germany.
Deutsche Dienststelle (WaSt), Berlin-Lichterfelde, Germany.
National Archives, College Park, MD, U.S.A.

Pre-1945 material
NARS microfilm collection A3343SS0 (partial Berlin Document Center Collection)"Dienstalterliste der Schultzstaffel der NSDAP," issues for 1934, 1935, 1936, 1937, 1938, 1939 (addendum), October 1942, November 1942, May 1943, October 1943, January 1944, July 1944, October 1944, and November 1944, SS-Personalamt.
Der Schwarze Korps (Periodical).
SS-Personalverordnungsblatt.
SS-Verordnungsblatt.
Verordnungsblatt der Waffen-SS.

Postwar material
Agte, Patrick. *Michael Wittmann erfolgreichster Panzerkommandant im Zweiten Weltkrieg*. Rosenheim, Germany: Deutsche Verlagsgesellschaft, 1994.
Agte, Patrick. *Jochen Peiper, Kommandeur Panzerregiment Leibstandarte*. Berg am Starnberger See, Germany: Kurt Vorwinckel-Verlag KG, 1998.
Angolia, John. *For Führer and Fatherland, Military Awards*. San Jose, California, U.S.A.: R. James Bender Publishing, 1976.
Bender, Roger James and Taylor, Hugh Page. *Uniforms, Organization and History of the Waffen-SS*. 5 volumes. San Jose, California, U.S.A.: R. James Bender Publishing, 1971-1983.
Munin Verlag GmbH. *Der Freiwillige*. Osnabrück, Germany (various issues).
Fellgiebel, Walter-Peer. *Die Träger des Ritterkreuzes des Eisernen Kreuzes 1939-1945*. Wölfersheim-Berstadt, Germany: Podzun-Pallas-Verlag GmbH, 1993.
Fischer, Thomas. *Von Berlin bis Caen – Entwicklung und Einsätze der Divisions-und Korps-Artillerie der LAH 1939-1945*. Aachen, Germany: Helios Verlags-und Buchvertriebsgesellschaft, 2004.
Fischer, Thomas. *Soldiers of the Leibstandarte*. Winnipeg, Canada: J.J. Fedorowicz Publishing, Inc., 2008.
Hanseatisches Auktionshaus für Historica. *80. Auktion Sonderkatalog mit dem Nachlass des SS-Brigadeführer und Generalmajor der Waffen-SS Theodor Wisch*. Bad Oldesloe, Germany: Hanseatisches Auktionshaus für Historica, 1997.
Hausser, Paul. *Soldaten wie andere auch*. Osnabrück, Germany: Munin Verlag GmbH, 1966.
Höhne, Heinz. *Der Orden unter dem Totenkopf – Die Geschichte der SS*. München, Germany: Bertelsmann Verlag GmbH, 1967.
Kameradschaft 1.Kompanie LAH. *Zwölf Jahre 1.Kompanie Leibstandarte SS Adolf Hitler, Ein Buch der Kameradschaft*. Rosenheim, Germany: Deutsche-Verlagsgesellschaft, 1990.
Keilig, Wolf. *Die Generale des Heeres*. Wölfersheim-Berstadt, Germany: Podzun-Pallas-Verlag GmbH, 1983.
Krätschmer, E.G. *Die Ritterkreuzträger der Waffen-SS*. Göttingen, Germany: Plesse Verlag K.W. Schütz, 1955.
Krausnick, Helmut. *Anatomy of the SS State*. Walker and Company, 1968.
Lehmann, Rudolf. *Die Leibstandarte*. Volume I – III. Osnabrück, Germany: Munin Verlag GmbH, 1977 – 1982.
Lehmann, Rudolf; Tiemann, Ralf. *Die Leibstandarte*. Volume IV/1, Osnabrück, Germany: Munin Verlag GmbH, 1986.
Lehmann, Rudolf. *Die Leibstandarte im Bild*. Coburg, Germany: Nation Europa Verlag, 1998.
Mooney, Peter. *Dietrich's Warrior's, The History of the 3.Kompanie/1. Panzergrenadier Regiment, 1.SS Panzer Division Leibstandarte Adolf Hitler in World War II*. Atglen, Pennsylvania: Schiffer Publishing Ltd., 2004.
Patzwall, Klaus and Scherzer, Veit. *Das Deutsche Kreuz 1941-1945*. Melbeck, Germany: Verlag Klaus D. Patzwall, 2001.
Rogmann, Willi. *Willi Rogmann Einzelkämpfer der Leibstandarte Träger der Nahkampfspange in Gold*. Bad Lobenstein, Germany: Militärfoto-Verlag Bethge, 2009.
Scheibert, Horst. *Ehrenblattspange, Ehrentafelspange, Ehrenpokale*. Wölfersheim-Berstadt, Germany: Podzun-Pallas-Verlag GmbH, 1986.
Schulz, Andreas / Zinke, Dieter. *Die Generale der Waffen-SS und Polizei 1939-1945*. Bissendorf, Germany: Biblio-Verlag, 2003
Schulze-Kossens, Richard. *Militärischer Führernachwuchs der Waffen-SS. Die Junkerschulen*. Osnabrück, Germany: Munin-Verlag GmbH, 1982.

Schumacher, Martin. *M.d.B. Volksvertretung im Wiederaufbau 1946-1961. Bundestagskandidaten und Mitglieder der westzonalen Vorparlamente. Eine biographische Dokumentation.* Düsseldorf, Germany: Droste Verlag, 2000.

Thiele, Hans-Günther. *Die Wehrmachtsaustellung – Dokumentation einer Kontroverse.* Bremen, Germany: Edition Temmen, 1997.

Trang, Charles. *Leibstandarte Archives.* Bayeux Cedex, France: Editions Heimdal, 2008.

Tiemann, Ralf. *Die Leibstandarte.* Volume IV/2. Osnabrück, Germany: Munin Verlag GmbH, 1987.

Walther, Herbert. *Die 1.SS-Panzer-Division Leibstandarte.* Wölfersheim-Berstadt, Germany: Podzun-Pallas-Verlag GmbH, without publication date.

Walther, Herbert. *Die 12.SS-Panzer-Division HJ.* Wölfersheim-Berstadt, Germany: Podzun-Pallas-Verlag GmbH, without publication date.

Yerger, Mark C. *Allgemeine-SS, The Commands, Units and Leaders of the General SS.* Atglen, Pennsylvania: Schiffer Publishing Ltd., 1997.

Yerger, Mark C. *German Cross in Silver Holders of the SS and Police.* San Jose, California, U.S.A.: R. James Bender Publishing, 2002.

Yerger, Mark C. *German Cross in Gold Holders of the SS and Police.* Volumes 1-4. San Jose, California, U.S.A.: R. James Bender Publishing, 2003-2008.

Yerger, Mark C. *Otto Weidinger, Knight's Cross with Oakleaves and Swords.* Atglen, Pennsylvania: Schiffer Publishing Ltd., 2000.

Yerger, Mark C. *Waffen-SS Commanders, The Army, Corps, and Divisional Leaders of a Legend.* (2 volumes) Atglen, Pennsylvania: Schiffer Publishing Ltd., 1998 and 1999.

Westemeier, Jens. *Joachim Peiper, A biography of Himmler's SS Commander.* Atglen, Pennsylvania: Schiffer Publishing Ltd., 2007.

(Above) March/April 1933: Eight of the first 117 volunteers at the Friesenstrasse barracks in Berlin-Kreuzberg, where the unit was first quartered. It later moved to the Kadettenanstalt in Berlin-Lichterfelde by the end of April that year: From left are Willi Montel, Rolf Picker, Hans Collani, Willi Riester, Theodor Wisch, Wilhelm Mohnke, Fritz Witt, and Hans von Stein. Montel saw combat with the "Leibstandarte" in 1941 before serving with the SS-Wachbatallion "Nordwest" in 1942 and the 13.Waffen-Gebirgs-Division in 1943; while still an Obersturmführer d.R. Riester was commissioned on April 20, 1937, after attending Junkerschule Braunschweig. He was killed on June 17, 1940, as Kompanie Chef of the 1./Der Führer. Promoted to Sturmbannführer on April 20, 1943, Hans von Stein transferred to the SS-WuVHA (SS-Economic and Administrative Main Office) the same year. Hans Collani served as adjutant to Sepp Dietrich during the prewar years and won the German Cross in Gold on April 24, 1944. He was killed leading SS-Freiwilligen-Panzer-Grenadier-Regiment "De Ruyter" at Narwa on July 29, 1944. For leading that regiment he was posthumously awarded the Knight's Cross on August 19, 1944, and promoted to Standartenführer. (Below) The Berlin-Lichterfelde "Leibstandarte" barracks. *Author's collection.*

Note in particular the early SS banner and one image where men are wearing SS runes on their exercise clothing. *Author's collection.*

Lehrsturm I - Tr.-Üb.-Pl. Zossen
3

Lehrsturm I - Tr.-Üb.-Pl. Zossen, 1933

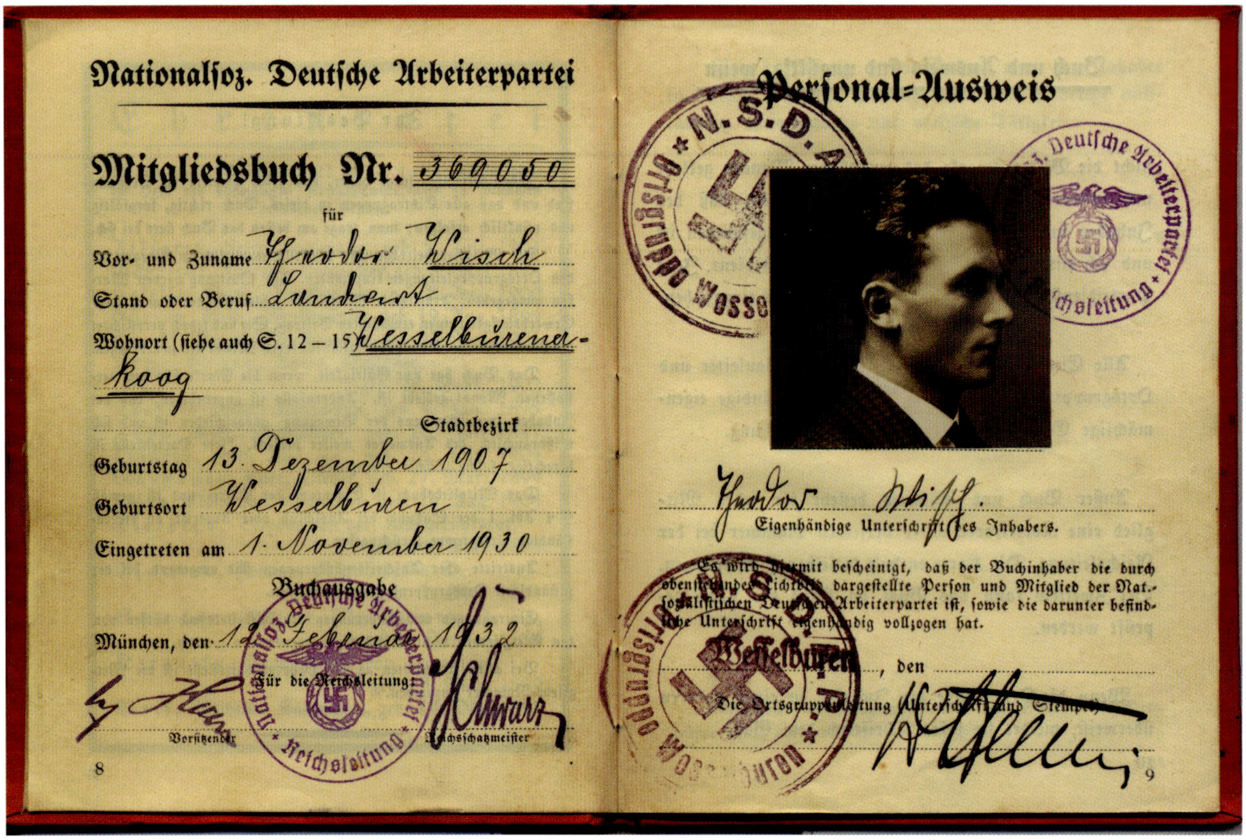
Nationalsoz. Deutsche Arbeiterpartei

Mitgliedsbuch Nr. 369050

für

Vor- und Zuname Theodor Wisch

Stand oder Beruf Landwirt

Wohnort (siehe auch S. 12 – 15) Wesselburener-Koog

Stadtbezirk

Geburtstag 13. Dezember 1907

Geburtsort Wesselburen

Eingetreten am 1. November 1930

Buchausgabe

München, den 12. Februar 1932

Für die Reichsleitung

Vorsitzender Reichsschatzmeister

8

Personal-Ausweis

Eigenhändige Unterschrift des Inhabers.

Es wird hiermit bescheinigt, daß der Buchinhaber die durch obenstehendes Lichtbild dargestellte Person und Mitglied der Nationalsozialistischen Deutschen Arbeiterpartei ist, sowie die darunter befindliche Unterschrift eigenhändig vollzogen hat.

Wesselburen, den

Die Ortsgruppenleitung (Unterschrift und Stempel)

9

Wisch's first issue NSDAP membership book, issued on February 12, 1932, in Munich. (Below) Page 13 confirms he joined the "Leibstandarte Adolf Hitler" on March 17, 1933, and was signed by Ortsgruppenleiter and Sturmführer Leroux, head of the NSDAP personnel department. *Author's collection.*

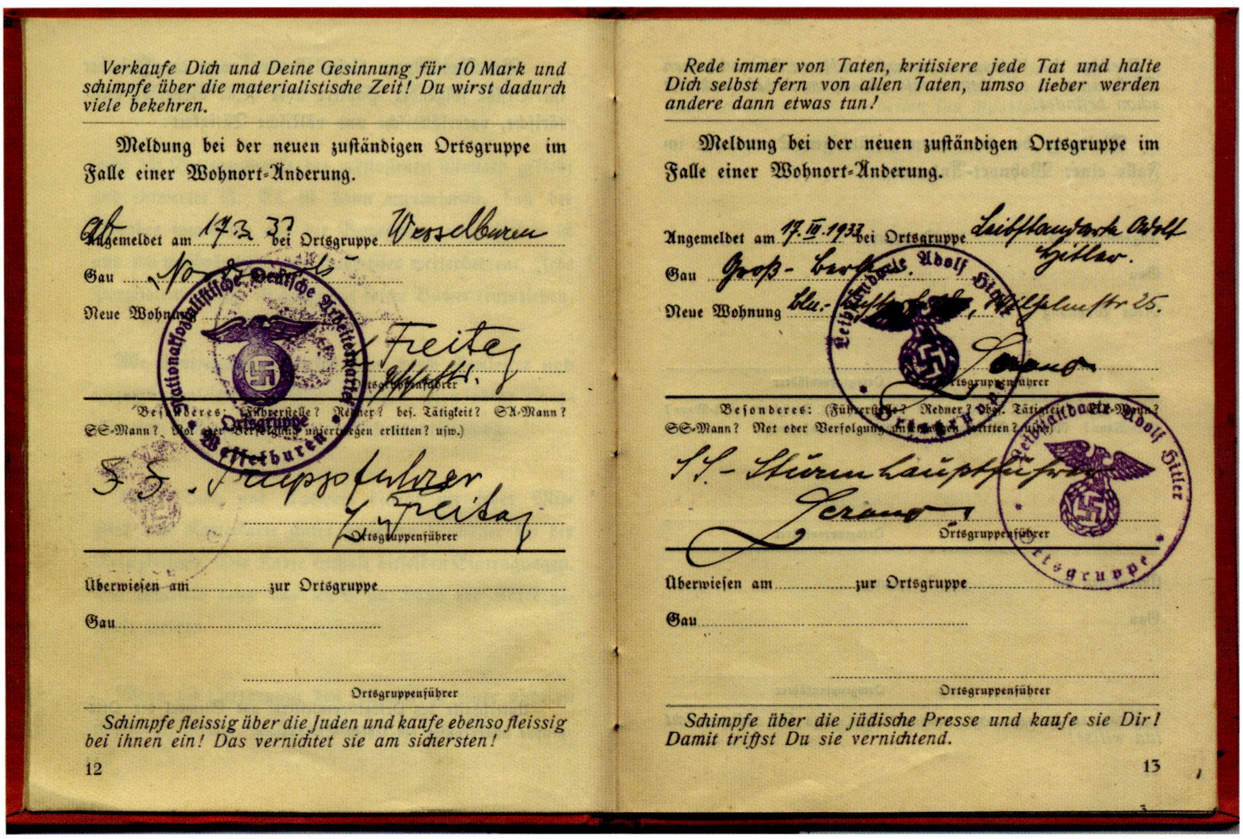
Verkaufe Dich und Deine Gesinnung für 10 Mark und schimpfe über die materialistische Zeit! Du wirst dadurch viele bekehren.

Meldung bei der neuen zuständigen Ortsgruppe im Falle einer Wohnort-Änderung.

Abgemeldet am 17.3.33 bei Ortsgruppe Wesselburen

Gau

Neue Wohnung

Besonderes: (Amtswalterstelle? Redner? bes. Tätigkeit? SA-Mann? SS-Mann? Not oder Verfolgung um der Bewegung willen erlitten? usw.)

SS-Truppführer

Ortsgruppenführer

Überwiesen am .... zur Ortsgruppe

Gau

Ortsgruppenführer

Schimpfe fleissig über die Juden und kaufe ebenso fleissig bei ihnen ein! Das vernichtet sie am sichersten!

12

Rede immer von Taten, kritisiere jede Tat und halte Dich selbst fern von allen Taten, umso lieber werden andere dann etwas tun!

Meldung bei der neuen zuständigen Ortsgruppe im Falle einer Wohnort-Änderung.

Angemeldet am 17.III.1933 bei Ortsgruppe Leibstandarte Adolf Hitler

Gau Groß-Berlin

Neue Wohnung

Ortsgruppenführer

Besonderes: (Führerstelle? Redner? bes. Tätigkeit? SA-Mann? SS-Mann? Not oder Verfolgung um der Bewegung willen erlitten? usw.)

SS-Sturmhauptführer

Ortsgruppenführer

Überwiesen am .... zur Ortsgruppe

Gau

Ortsgruppenführer

Schimpfe über die jüdische Presse und kaufe sie Dir! Damit triffst Du sie vernichtend.

13

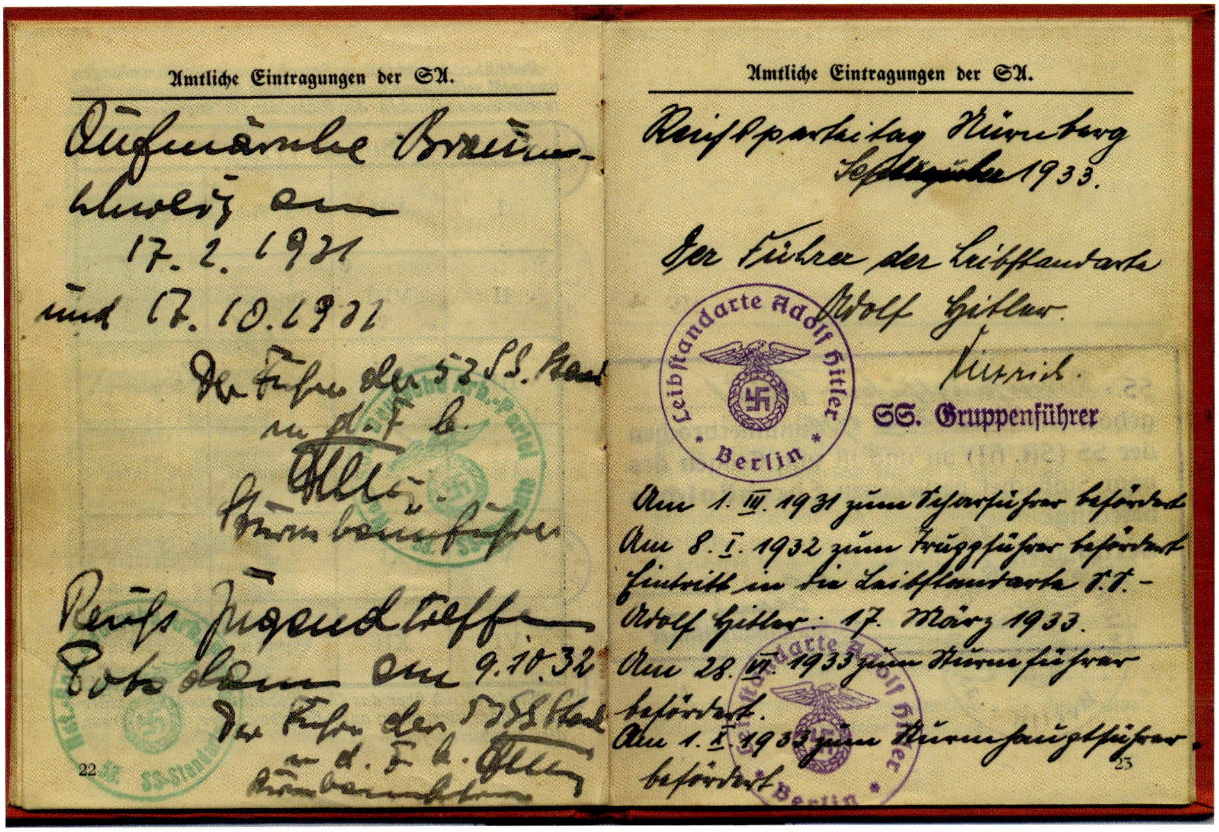

Amtliche Eintragungen der SA.

22

Amtliche Eintragungen der SA.

SS. Gruppenführer

23

Pages 22-23 show Wisch attended the 1931 and 1932 NSDAP rallies in Braunschweig, a Reichsjugendtreffen in Potsdam on October 9, 1932, and the September 1933 Reichsparteitag in Nürnberg (signed by Sepp Dietrich). Page 23 has Wisch's promotions and joining the "Leibstandarte" on March 17, 1933. Page 24 confirms his promotion to Sturmhauptführer on October 1, 1933, and authorization to wear the SS dagger due to early SS membership. *Author's collection.*

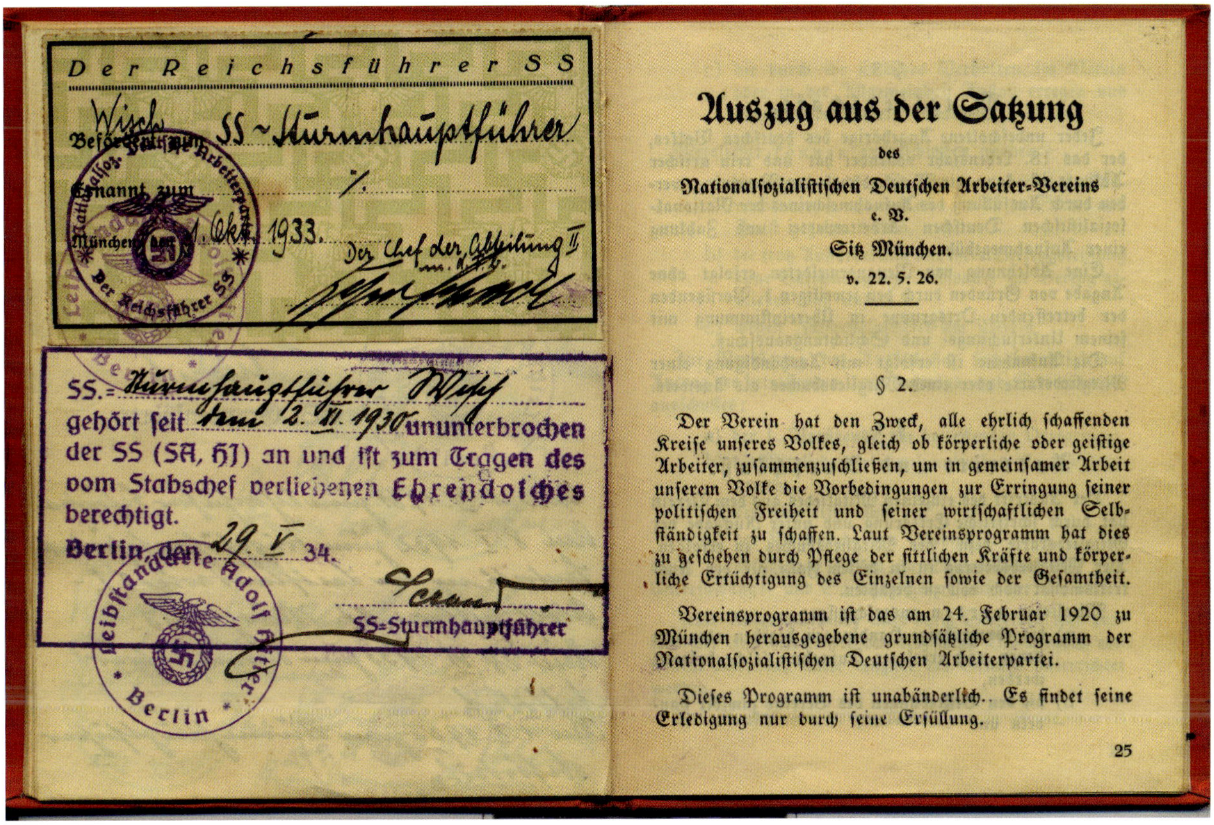

Der Reichsführer SS

Befördert zum SS-Sturmhauptführer

Ernannt zum

München, den 1. Okt. 1933.

SS.= Sturmhauptführer Wisch gehört seit dem 2. VI. 1930 ununterbrochen der SS (SA, HJ) an und ist zum Tragen des vom Stabschef verliehenen Ehrendolches berechtigt.

Berlin, den 29. V. 34.

SS-Sturmhauptführer

Auszug aus der Satzung

des

Nationalsozialistischen Deutschen Arbeiter-Vereins

e. V.

Sitz München.

v. 22. 5. 26.

§ 2.

Der Verein hat den Zweck, alle ehrlich schaffenden Kreise unseres Volkes, gleich ob körperliche oder geistige Arbeiter, zusammenzuschließen, um in gemeinsamer Arbeit unserem Volke die Vorbedingungen zur Erringung seiner politischen Freiheit und seiner wirtschaftlichen Selbständigkeit zu schaffen. Laut Vereinsprogramm hat dies zu geschehen durch Pflege der sittlichen Kräfte und körperliche Ertüchtigung des Einzelnen sowie der Gesamtheit.

Vereinsprogramm ist das am 24. Februar 1920 zu München herausgegebene grundsätzliche Programm der Nationalsozialistischen Deutschen Arbeiterpartei.

Dieses Programm ist unabänderlich.. Es findet seine Erledigung nur durch seine Erfüllung.

25

Above: Hauptsturmführer Wisch (center) and fellow comrades in a group photo after attending a funeral. All wear black straps above their NSDAP armbands. Right: Eventual Oberscharführer Waldemar Heinrich, shown wearing prewar "Totenkopf" insignia, was Theodor Wisch's half-brother from his father's relationship after the death of Frau Wisch. Heinrich originally served with the "Totenkopf" Division before being transferred to the "Leibstandarte" in early 1943. *Author's collection.*

Wisch as a young Hauptsturmführer wearing his Sports Badge and Old Fighter's Chevron on his right sleeve, indicating pre-1933 SS membership. *Author's collection.*

Above: Wisch seen here as a young Hauptsturmführer wearing a light grey open collar tunic during an outing on horseback in the pre-war years. Below: Wisch and his 1.Kompanie in a group photo after their June/July 1935 stay at the Hammelburg infantry training facility. *Author's collection.*

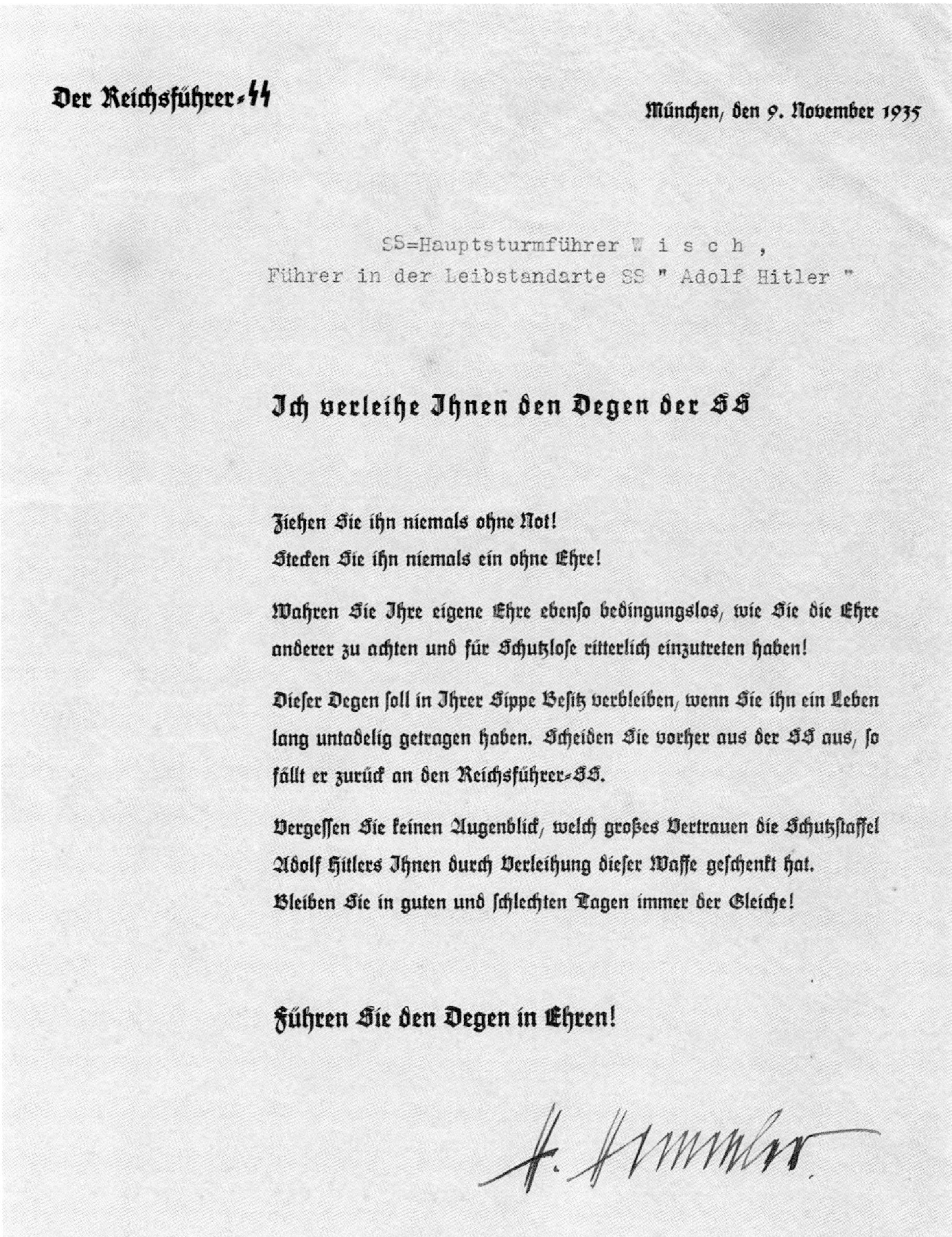

Der Reichsführer-SS

München, den 9. November 1935

SS=Hauptsturmführer W i s c h ,
Führer in der Leibstandarte SS " Adolf Hitler "

Ich verleihe Ihnen den Degen der SS

Ziehen Sie ihn niemals ohne Not!
Stecken Sie ihn niemals ein ohne Ehre!

Wahren Sie Ihre eigene Ehre ebenso bedingungslos, wie Sie die Ehre anderer zu achten und für Schutzlose ritterlich einzutreten haben!

Dieser Degen soll in Ihrer Sippe Besitz verbleiben, wenn Sie ihn ein Leben lang untadelig getragen haben. Scheiden Sie vorher aus der SS aus, so fällt er zurück an den Reichsführer-SS.

Vergessen Sie keinen Augenblick, welch großes Vertrauen die Schutzstaffel Adolf Hitlers Ihnen durch Verleihung dieser Waffe geschenkt hat.
Bleiben Sie in guten und schlechten Tagen immer der Gleiche!

Führen Sie den Degen in Ehren!

H. Himmler

As a Hauptsturmführer Wisch was awarded his SS sword. The document is dated November 9, 1935, and was signed by Heinrich Himmler. *Private collection.*

Above: The rally from June 28 to July 3, 1936, in Weimar celebrated the tenth anniversary of the NSDAP. From left are Robert Arthecker (ended the war as a Hauptsturmführer with SS-Panzer-Grenadier-Regiment 88 and died in Bergneustadt on October 18, 1980), Siegfried Lange, Bernhard Herber (killed as an Untersturmführer with SS-Panzer-Grenadier-Regiment 1 on February 10, 1943, in Rogan, Russia), Willi Schütt, Willi Frigger, Hermann Hammersen, Theodor Wisch (back to camera), Eitel Borck (as a Hauptsturmführer was later Kompanie Chef of the 1./Polizei Bataillon 66), Martin Weigelt, Heinrich Piel, Gerhard Straubel (as a Hauptsturmführer ended the war as Batterie Chef of the 5./SS-Flak Abteilung 1 and died on March 14, 1991), and Siegfried Böker. Note the famous 1923 Munich putsch carried "Blutfahne" (Blood Flag) on the far right. Below: Hauptsturmführer Theodor Wisch with eight of his men wearing white leather gear are standing in front of the entrance to one of the buildings at the Berlin-Lichterfelde barracks. *Author's collection.*

Above: Hauptsturmführer Herbert Kaschula, Kompanie Chef of the 20./LSSAH, is briefed by Wisch (then commander of the V./LSSAH) during a training exercise at the Lichterfelde barracks in 1941. Next to Wisch are (from left) Hauptscharführer Herbert Schnelle (Platoon Leader with the 20./LSSAH) and Unterscharführer Janssen (Group Leader in the 20./LSSAH). Schnelle was later commissioned and briefly commanded the I./SS-Panzer-Grenadier-Regiment 2 as a Hauptsturmführer in 1944 after leading the 5.Kompanie. He died on March 23, 1995. Kaschula later led the 5./SS-Panzer-Grenadier-Regiment 2, and as a Sturmbannführer eventually commanded the VII./LSSAH in 1944. Below: "Leibstandarte SS Adolf Hitler 1.Kompanie." The Kompanie designation was drawn in the sand by men during an outing to Schmolsin, on the Baltic Sea, in 1937. *Author's collection.*

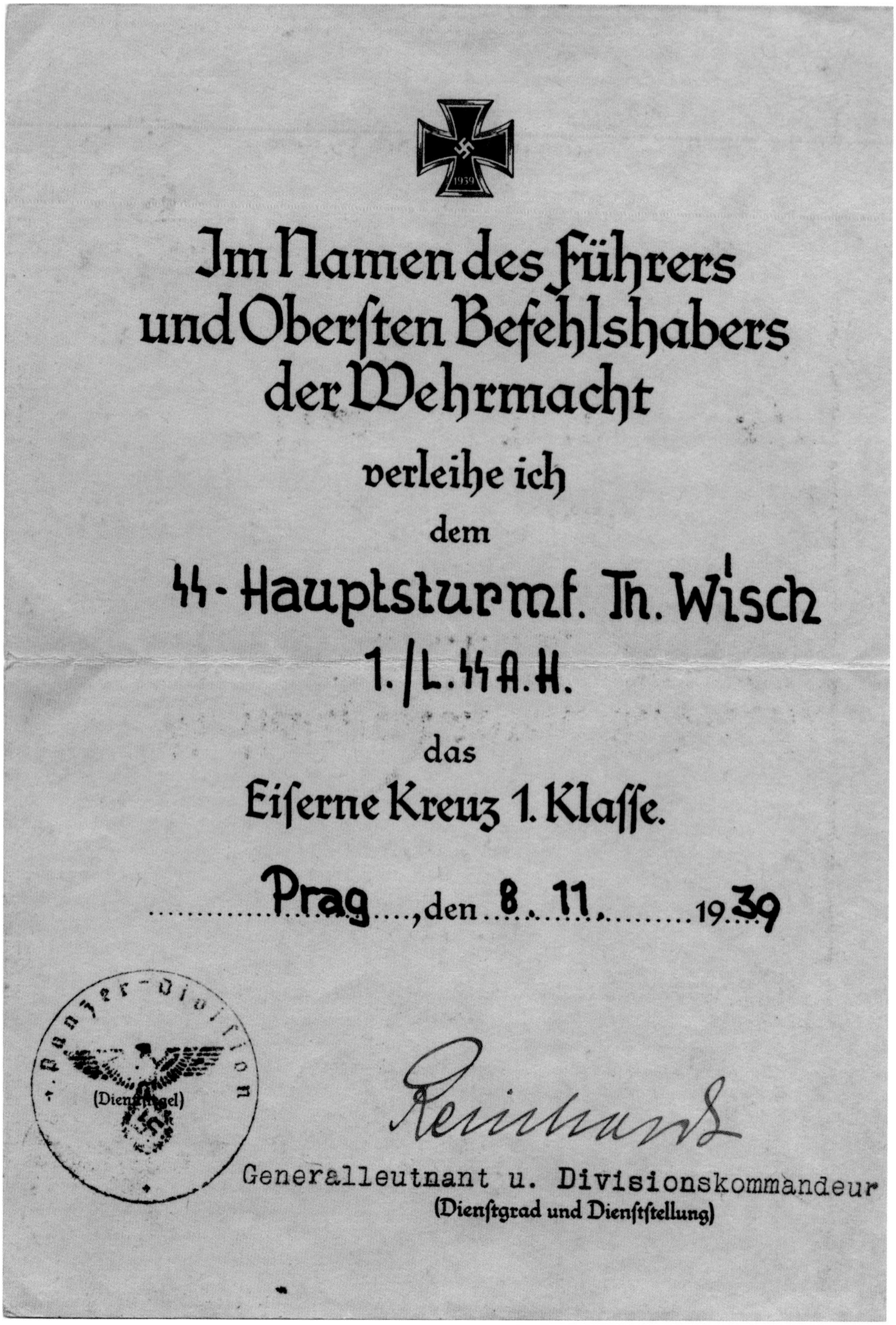

1939

Im Namen des Führers
und Oberſten Befehlshabers
der Wehrmacht

verleihe ich

dem

SS-Hauptsturmf. Th. Wisch
1./L.SSA.H.

das

Eiſerne Kreuz 1. Klaſſe.

Prag, den 8. 11. 1939

Generalleutnant u. Divisionskommandeur
(Dienſtgrad und Dienſtſtellung)

Wisch's award document for the Iron Cross First Class dated November 11, 1939, earned leading the 1.Kompanie "LSSAH" during the Polish campaign. The document was signed by Generalleutnant Reinhardt, commander of the 4.Panzer-Armee, to which the "Leibstandarte" was attached. *Author's collection.*

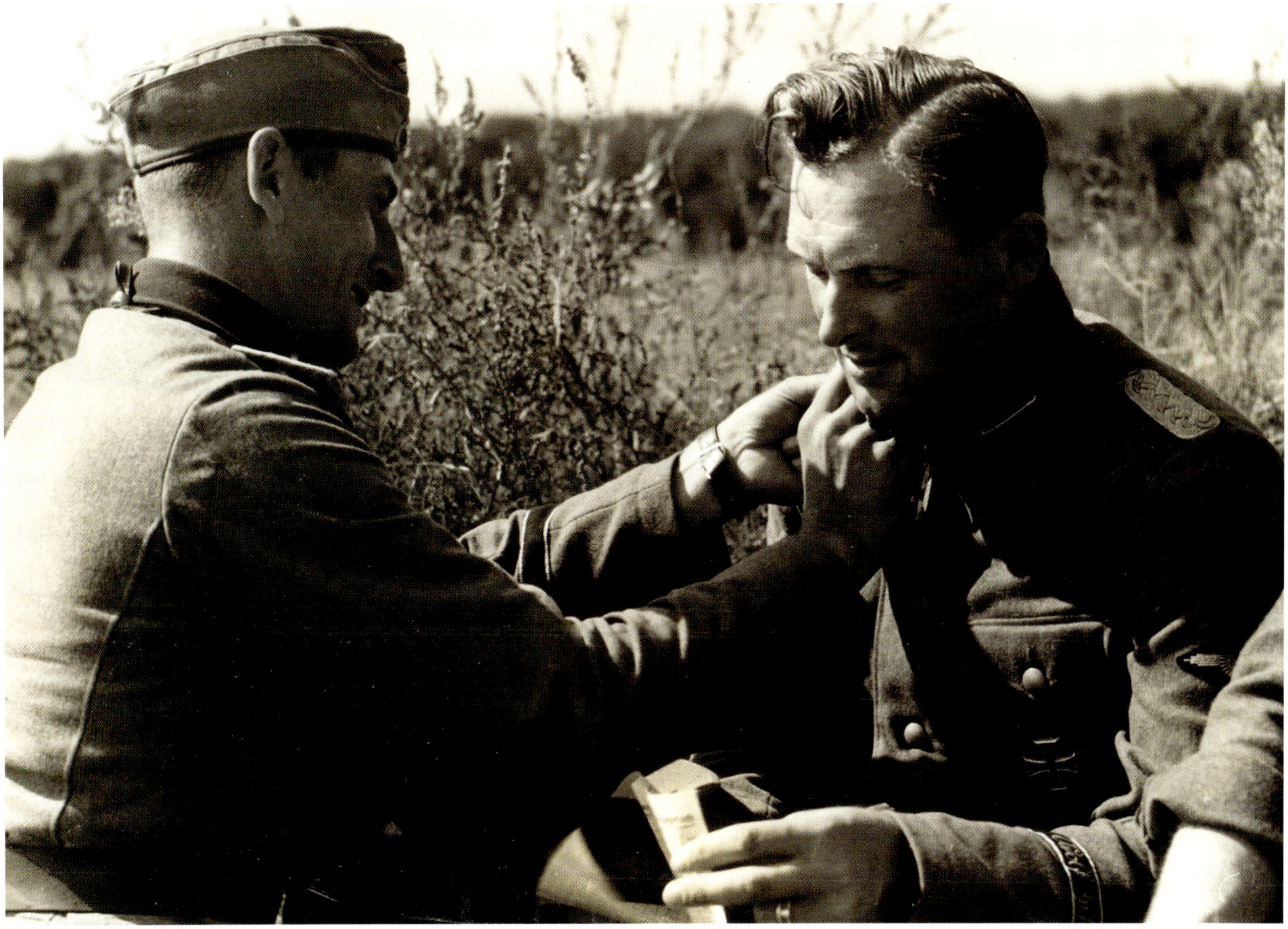

Above: September 19, 1941: With two quickly improvised safety pins Hauptsturmführer Hans Scappini attaches a converted Iron Cross 2nd Class as a substitute for the unavailable Knight's Cross to Wisch's collar. Note that Wisch still holds the radio message with the notification of the award in his left hand (See original message illustration). Right: Wearing his field cap to protect him against the sun, Wisch is wearing his recently awarded Knight's Cross. *Author's collection.*

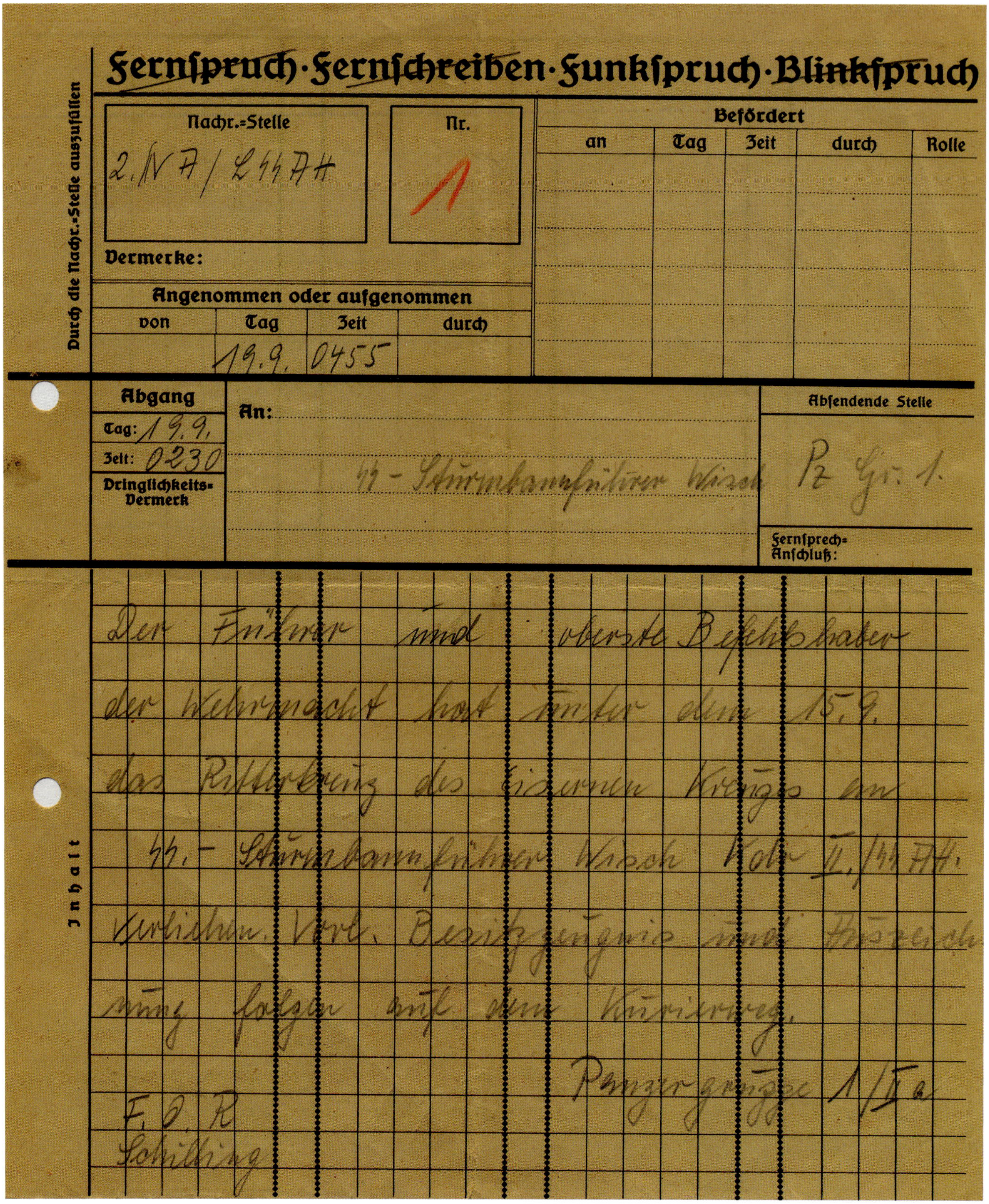
Fernspruch · Fernschreiben · Funkspruch · Blinkspruch

Nachr.-Stelle: 2./N7/LSSAH
Nr.: 1
Vermerke:

Befördert: an | Tag | Zeit | durch | Rolle

Angenommen oder aufgenommen: von | Tag 19.9. | Zeit 0455 | durch

Abgang — Tag: 19.9. — Zeit: 0230
Dringlichkeits-Vermerk

An: SS-Sturmbannführer Wisch

Absendende Stelle: Pz Gr. 1
Fernsprech-Anschluß:

Inhalt:

Der Führer und oberste Befehlshaber der Wehrmacht hat unter dem 15.9. das Ritterkreuz des Eisernen Kreuzes an SS-Sturmbannführer Wisch Kdr. II./SS AH. verliehen. Vorl. Besitzzeugnis und Auszeichnung folgen auf dem Kurierweg.

Panzergruppe 1/IIa

F.d.R.
Schilling

Durch die Nachr.-Stelle auszufüllen

The original radio message Wisch received from Panzergruppe 1 (Generalfeldmarschall Ewald von Kleist), notifying him of the Knight's Cross awarded to him by the Supreme Commander of the Wehrmacht, Adolf Hitler (see text). *Author's collection.*

Top: Wisch wearing his field tunic and newly awarded Knight's Cross. Note he rarely wore his award on a neck ribbon, usually only attaching the Cross's loop to the hooks of his tunic's neck closure. Below: Wisch was euphorically received by the people of Heide/Holstein after winning the Knight's Cross for combat in Russia. Local SS, SA, Hitlerjugend, and BDM formations were also present during the occasion. *Author's collection.*

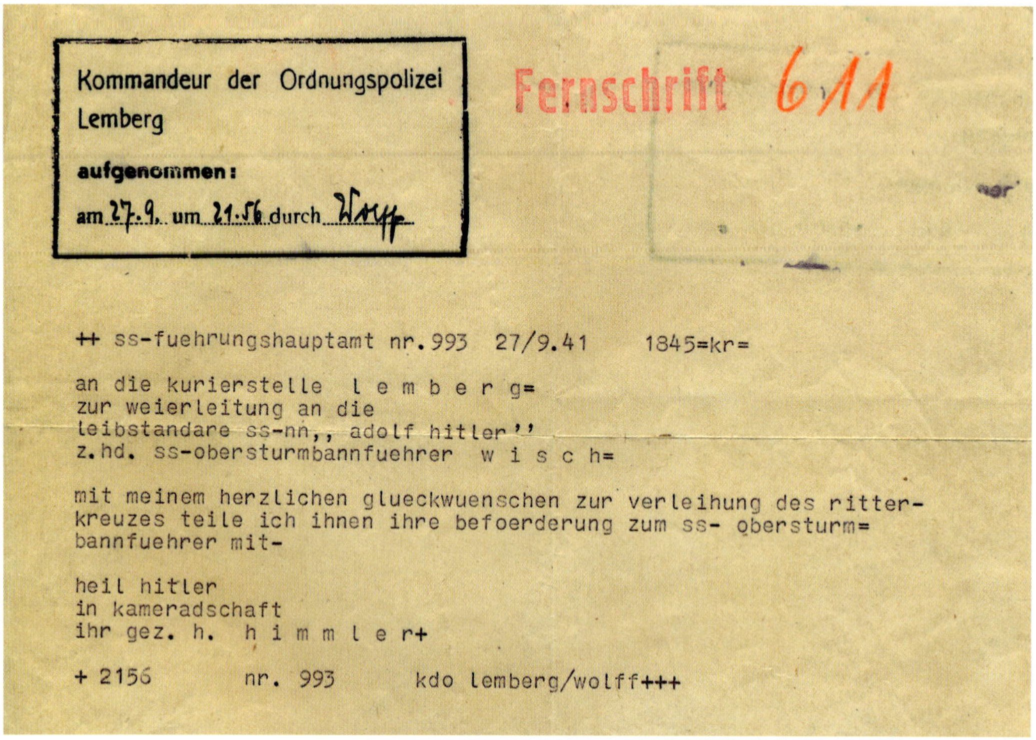

Kommandeur der Ordnungspolizei
Lemberg
aufgenommen:
am 27.9. um 21.56 durch Wolff

Fernschrift 6/11

++ ss-fuehrungshauptamt nr.993 27/9.41 1845=kr=

an die kurierstelle l e m b e r g=
zur weierleitung an die
leibstandare ss-nn,, adolf hitler''
z.hd. ss-obersturmbannfuehrer w i s c h=

mit meinem herzlichen glueckwuenschen zur verleihung des ritter-
kreuzes teile ich ihnen ihre befoerderung zum ss- obersturm=
bannfuehrer mit-

heil hitler
in kameradschaft
ihr gez. h. h i m m l e r+

+ 2156 nr. 993 kdo lemberg/wolff+++

Above: September 27, 1941: "With cordial congratulations on the award of the Knight's Cross, I notify you of your promotion to SS-Obersturmbannführer. Heil Hitler. In comradeship, Yours, signed H. Himmler." Note this Führungshauptamt document passed through the Ordnungspolizei command office in Lemberg before given to Wisch. Below: Congratulatory telegram from September 25, 1941: "I am sincerely pleased about the award of the Knight's Cross to you dear Wisch and congratulate you cordially on this high and well-earned award. Heil Hitler. Wolff." Karl Wolff (who also signed twice on the upper document) was Himmler's long time personal adjutant before heading his Personal Staff and then the Main Office it became, ending the war as Supreme SS and Police Leader in Italy. *Author's collection.*

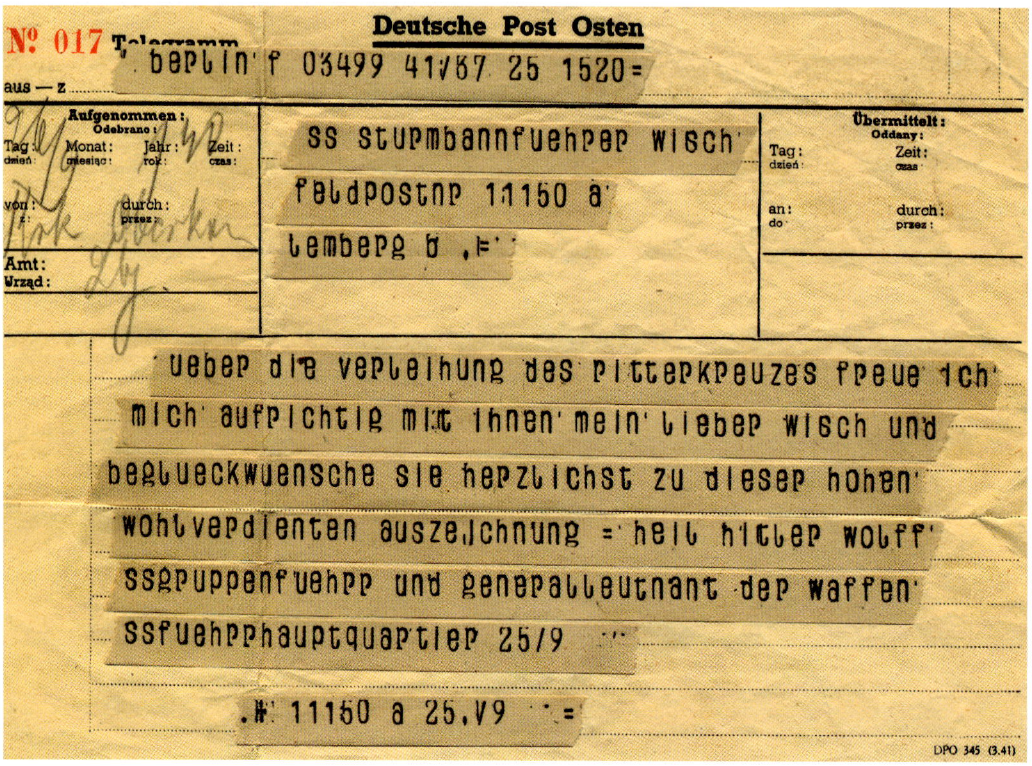

Nº 017 Telegramm
Deutsche Post Osten
berlin f 03499 41/67 25 1520=
aus — z

Aufgenommen: Odebrano:
Tag: dzień: Monat: miesiąc: Jahr: rok: Zeit: czas:
von: z: durch: przez:
Amt: Urząd:

ss sturmbannfuehrer wisch
feldpostnr 11150 a
lemberg b ,F

Übermittelt: Oddany:
Tag: dzień: Zeit: czas:
an: do: durch: przez:

ueber die verleihung des ritterkreuzes freue ich
mich aufrichtig mit ihnen mein lieber wisch und
begluecKwuensche sie herzlichst zu dieser hohen
wohlverdienten auszeichnung = heil hitler wolff
ssgruppenfuehrr und generalleutnant der waffen
ssfuehrrhauptquartier 25/9

.F 11150 a 25.V9 =

DPO 345 (3.41)

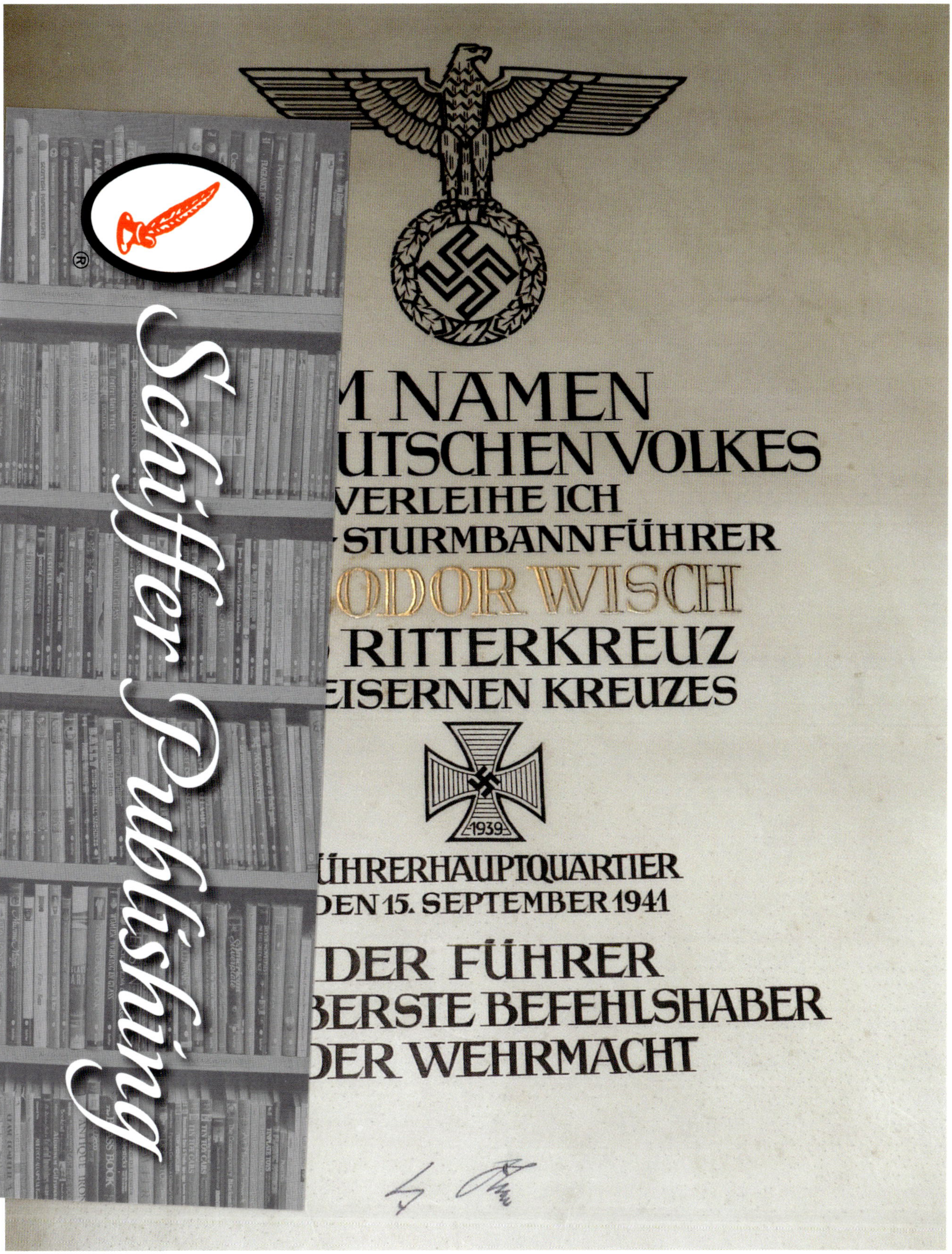

Theodor Wisch was one of the first soldiers of the German Wehrmacht to be awarded the Knight's Cross of the Iron Cross, and one of the very few soldiers to receive the formal handmade award document and leather folder. *Private collection.*

Wisch and fellow officers enjoy a rare special occasion meal, including a bottle of champagne, during a rest behind the front. Below: Fritz Wisch's grave marker (far right). Theodor Wisch's brother was an Oberscharführer in the 17./LSSAH and a holder of the NSDAP Service Medal in Bronze and Silver. He was killed at the Rollbahn "Nord" on July 17, 1941, leaving behind his wife Berta and sons Fritz, Heinz, and Uwe. *Author's collection.*

Sepp Dietrich (center) being briefed by his unit commanders. Sitting behind in assault gun uniform and overseas cap is Sturmbannführer Georg Schönberger (SS# 1 351), at the time Sturmgeschütz Batterie Chef. He won the German Cross in Gold on December 26, 1941, as commander of the Sturmgeschütz Abteilung for earlier combats and the Knight's Cross posthumously on December 20, 1943, as an Obersturmbannführer commanding SS-Panzer-Regiment 1. Standing in the back with the Knight's Cross is Hauptsturmführer Gerd Pleiss (SS# 323 807), a prewar Junkerschule Braunschweig graduate, who had won his award on April 20, 1941, commanding the 1.Kompanie at Klidi-Pass. Severely wounded on November 17, 1941, he died the same day at the Hauptverbandsplatz of 2.Santiäts Kompanie "LAH," near Taganrog. Further right are Hauptsturmführer Max Wünsche and Sturmbannführer Alexander Sukkau (SS# 260 660), commander of the I./Artillerie Regiment. Sukkau ended the war commanding the SS-Artillerie Regiment 7 of the 7.SS-Gebirgsdivision "Prinz Eugen." Standartenführer Walter Staudinger (SS# 242 652), commander of the Artillerie Regiment, sits with back to the camera wearing a camouflage smock. Staudinger served with Bayerische Gebrigsbatterie 10 during World War I, joining the police and the NSDAP in Munich in 1920. Due to his participation in the November 9, 1923, Putsch with Kampfbund München, he was suspended from police duty and his membership to the NSDAP was prohibited. By 1934, as a Sturmbannführer, he was an adjutant with Himmler and later with Reinhard Heydrich. Staudinger became Höherer Artillerie Kommandeur of Panzer Armee Oberkommando 6 at the start of October 1944 and was promoted to Gruppenführer on November 11, 1944. He died on August 31, 1964. Left of Dietrich stands Theodor Wisch wearing an M43 cap, and in front of Dietrich sitting to the left is Kurt "Panzer" Meyer, then commander of the Reconnaissance Detachment. Gustav Mertsch (SS# 183 351) can be seen standing on the far left of the photo wearing binoculars. Mertsch served with the Reichswehr from 1919 in artillery and Flak units. He entered the SS-VT Artillerie Regiment as a Hauptsturmführer on June 6, 1939, taking command of the II./Artillerie Regiment "LSSAH" as a Sturmbannführer on September 1, 1940. Mertsch was promoted to Obersturmbannführer on April 20, 1943, and won the German Cross in Gold on September 2, 1943, as commander of the IV./Artillerie Regiment. He died on February 7, 1986. *Author's Collection.*

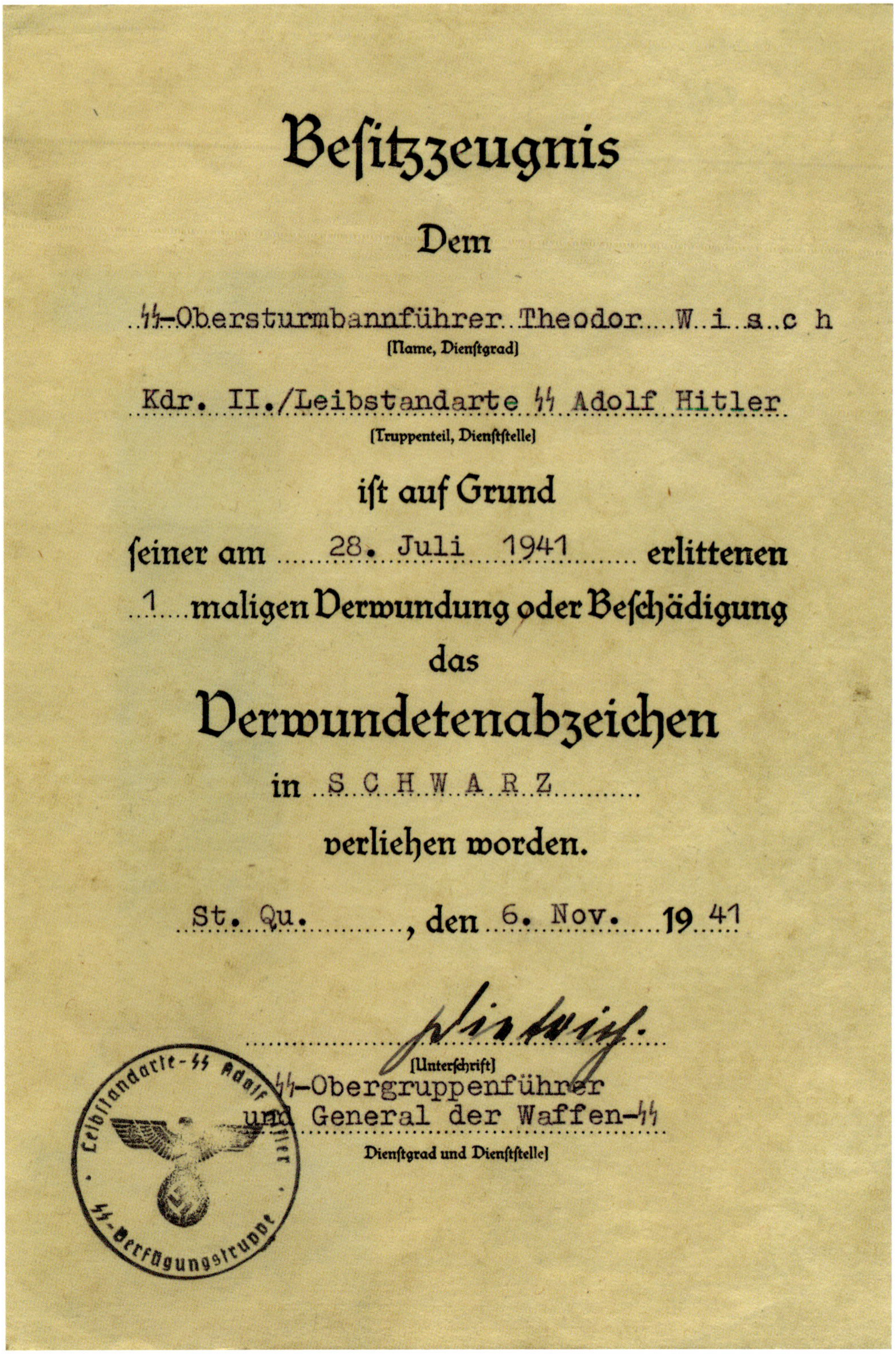

Besitzzeugnis

Dem

SS-Obersturmbannführer Theodor W i s c h
(Name, Dienstgrad)

Kdr. II./Leibstandarte SS Adolf Hitler
(Truppenteil, Dienststelle)

ist auf Grund

seiner am 28. Juli 1941 erlittenen

1 maligen Verwundung oder Beschädigung

das

Verwundetenabzeichen

in S C H W A R Z

verliehen worden.

St. Qu., den 6. Nov. 1941

(Unterschrift)

SS-Obergruppenführer
und General der Waffen-SS
Dienstgrad und Dienststelle)

Leibstandarte-SS Adolf Hitler
SS-Verfügungstruppe

As a battalion commander at Rollbahn Nord, Wisch was awarded the Wound Badge in Black on July 28, 1941, by Obergruppenführer Sepp Dietrich. He also signed the document as commander of the "Leibstandarte." *Author's collection.*

Theodor Wisch (third from left), Max Wünsche (reading the "Illustrierter Beobachter"), and Sepp Dietrich enjoy a couple of hours of rest at a lake after weeks of combat. Below: Sepp Dietrich's command vehicle races ahead of the long march column at Rollbahn "Nord" during July 1941. Note the license plate "SS-501." *Courtesy of Thomas Fischer.*

Josef "Jupp" Diefenthal (SS # 283 050) was born on October 5, 1915, in Euskirchen. He joined the "Leibstandarte" on October 15, 1935, after finishing his Abitur. Before being promoted to Unterscharführer on November 9, 1938, and Oberscharführer on April 20, 1940, he had served as group and platoon leader. Diefenthal won the Iron Cross 2nd Class on September 24, 1939, and 1st Class on June 8, 1940. He was commissioned to Untersturmführer d.R. on September 1, 1940. Promoted to Obersturmführer d.R. on September 6, 1941, he served as battalion and later regimental adjutant alongside Theodor Wisch during the first two campaigns of the "Leibstandarte" in the East. On April 20, 1943, Diefenthal was promoted to Hauptsturmführer d.R. and given command of the 1.Kompanie. Later, leading III.(gep.)/SS-Panzergrenadier-Regiment 2, he was awarded the German Cross in Gold on October 29, 1944, and the Knight's Cross on February 5, 1945, following a recommendation by Obersturmbannführer Joachim Peiper on December 26, 1944. Josef Diefenthal died on April 13, 2001, in Euskirchen. *Courtesy of Tim Willemsen and Mark C. Yerger.* Below: Max Wünsche and Sepp Dietrich are thoroughly studying maps for the next attack. *Author's collection.*

IM NAMEN DES FÜHRERS
UND
OBERSTEN BEFEHLSHABERS
DER WEHRMACHT
IST DEM

SS-Brigadeführer und
Generalmajor der Waffen-SS
Theodor W i s c h
1. SS-Panzer-Division "LSSAH"
AM 25. Aug. 42

DIE MEDAILLE
WINTERSCHLACHT IM OSTEN
1941/42
(OSTMEDAILLE)
VERLIEHEN WORDEN.

Waffen-SS · Leibstandarte SS „Adolf Hitler"

FÜR DIE RICHTIGKEIT:

SS-Oberstgruppenführer und
Generaloberst der Waffen-SS

Wisch was awarded the Eastern Front Medal on August 25, 1942, for his participation in the winter campaign of 1941/42. Note that he was already a Brigadeführer and the commander of the "Leibstandarte" at the time the document was retroactively issued and signed by Oberstgruppenführer Sepp Dietrich. *Author's collection.*

Sepp Dietrich (second from left) poses with three officers he just decorated on behalf of the Kingdom of Romania. Fritz Witt (far left) was awarded the Order of the Star of Romania for Knights. Walter Staudinger (second from right) received the Star of Romania for Commanders, and Theodor Wisch the Order of the Crown of Romania with Swords for Officers. Staudinger also wears the white Bulgarian Order for Bravery (3rd class, 1st grade) next to his Iron Cross. Below: Sepp Dietrich presents Wisch with his corresponding award document. *Courtesy of Charles Trang.*

Above: Wisch gives Sturmbannführer Joachim Peiper, the commander of the III.(Armored)/SS-Panzer- Grenadier-Regiment 2 "LSSAH," new orders for the attack towards Kharkov during February 1943. Peiper is seen here wearing his Iron Cross First Class, won for fighting near Torcy, France, on June 13, 1940, leading the 11./LSSAH as a Hauptsturmführer. *Courtesy of Mark C. Yerger*. Below: In the evening of March 6, 1943, Wisch visited Peiper at his command post near Federowka, Russia. On the far right, Hauptsturmführer Paul Guhl is seen studying maps and passing orders by telephone. Guhl later won the German Cross in Gold on December 30, 1943, and the Knight's Cross on June 4, 1944, leading III./(Armored) SS-Panzer-Grenadier-Regiment 2. *Courtesy of Solkors-Collection.*

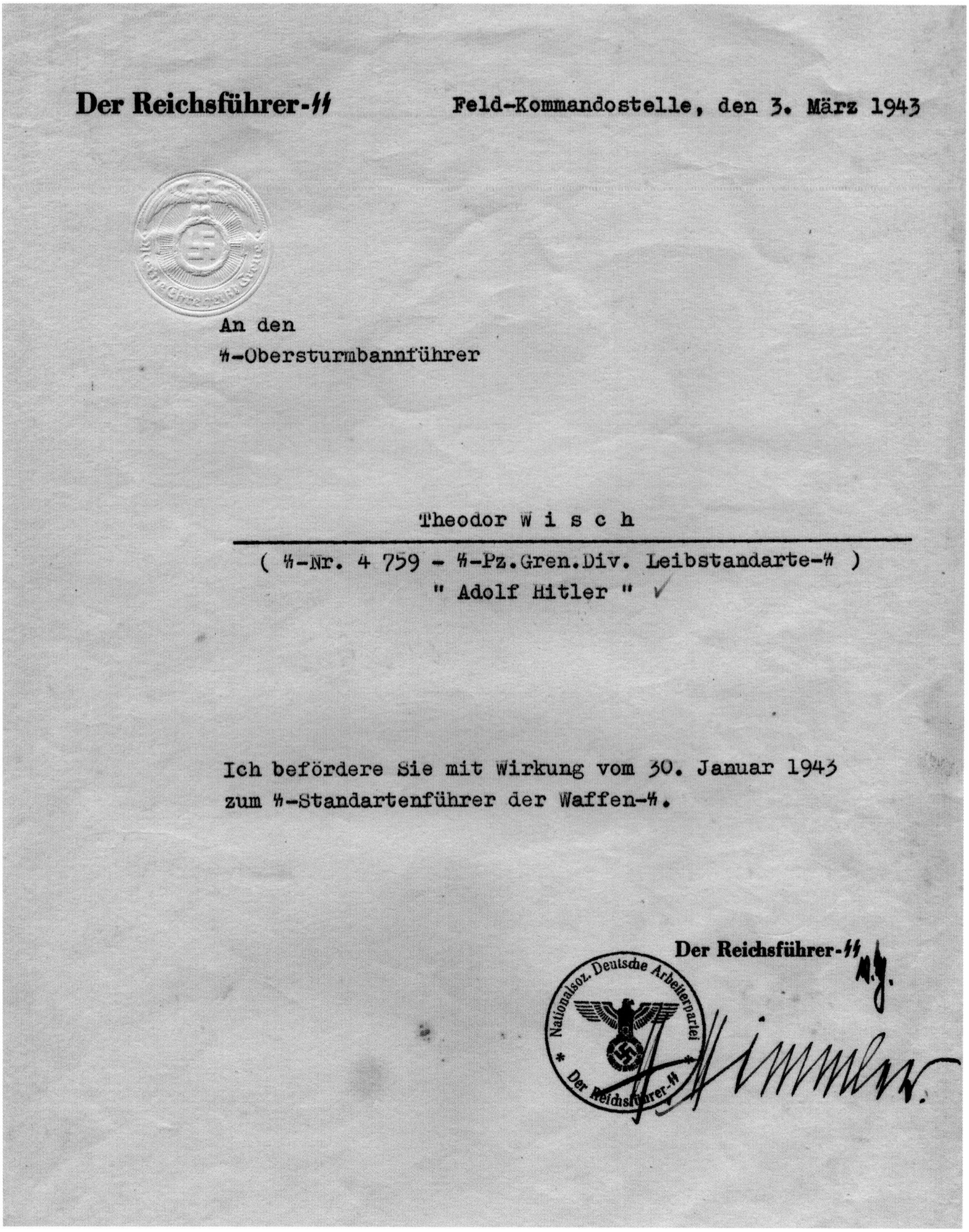

Der Reichsführer-SS Feld-Kommandostelle, den 3. März 1943

An den
SS-Obersturmbannführer

Theodor W i s c h

(SS-Nr. 4 759 - SS-Pz.Gren.Div. Leibstandarte-SS)
" Adolf Hitler "

Ich befördere Sie mit Wirkung vom 30. Januar 1943
zum SS-Standartenführer der Waffen-SS.

Der Reichsführer-SS

H. Himmler

Reichsführer-SS Heinrich Himmler signed this promotion document to SS-Standartenführer on March 3, 1943, effective January 30, 1943. *Author's collection.*

From left are Rudolf Sandig, Wisch, Hugo Kraas, and Hans Becker in a photo at Sepp Dietrich's 51st birthday celebration in Kharkov. Sandig and Kraas wear the rarely seen Bulgarian Bravery Order 4th grade, 1st class, awarded to them in February 1942. Becker was born on November 5, 1911, in Peenemünde, and was then leading the 2./SS-Panzer-Grenadier-Regiment 2. He won the Knight's Cross on March 28, 1943, from a proposal submitted by Wisch, and was killed in St. Lambert in the Falaise fighting on August 20, 1944, leading the I./SS-Panzer-Grenadier-Regiment 2. Hugo Kraas was born on January 25, 1911, in Witten an der Ruhr. He joined the SS/VT on October 15, 1935, serving in the 1.Sturm of the eventual Regiment "Germania" until attending the 1937 Junkerschule Braunschweig class. Commissioned on March 12, 1938, he was posted to the 7./LSSAH at the start of April. Promoted to Obersturmführer on April 20, 1939, Kraas was a platoon leader with Kurt "Panzer" Meyer's 14.(Panzerabwehr)/Kompanie in Poland. Following Meyer to the 15.(Kradschützen)/Kompanie, he won the Iron Cross 1st Class in the Western campaign. After the Reconnaissance Detachment was formed, Kraas was given command of its 2.Kompanie. Promoted to Hauptsturmführer on September 1, 1940, he was wounded in late July 1941 by artillery, returning to duty in Russia that October, and was awarded his German Cross in Gold on December 25, 1941. After deputizing for Kurt Meyer, Kraas next commanded the V./LSSAH from mid-February 1942, leading it at Leningrad. Promoted to Sturmbannführer on April 20, 1942, he led a redesignated I./Panzer-Grenadier-Regiment 2 at Kharkov and won the Knight's Cross on March 28, 1943. Kraas was chosen as Wisch's successor to command SS-Panzer-Genadier-Regiment 2. Wounded again on January 5, 1944, he won the Oakleaves on January 24, 1944. Following a divisional commander course in Hirschberg, Kraas took formal command of the 12.SS-Panzer-Division "Hitlerjugend" on November 19, 1944, and led it to the end of the war. Promoted to Oberführer on January 30, 1945, and to Brigadeführer on April 20, 1945, he was released from American captivity in 1948. Hugo Kraas died of a heart attack in Selk, Schleswig-Holstein, on February 20, 1980. *Author's collection.*

IM NAMEN DES FÜHRERS
UND OBERSTEN BEFEHLSHABERS
DER WEHRMACHT
VERLEIHE ICH
DEM
SS-STANDARTENFÜHRER
THEODOR WISCH
KOMMANDEUR 2.PZ.GR.RGT. „L.SS-A.H."
DAS DEUTSCHE KREUZ
IN GOLD

HAUPTQUARTIER, DEN 25. FEBRUAR 1943

OBERKOMMANDO DES HEERES

Keitel

GENERALFELDMARSCHALL

Theodor Wisch, then commanding SS-Panzer-Grenadier-Regiment 2, was awarded the German Cross in Gold for the weeks of combat leading to the recapture of Kharkov. The document was issued on February 25, 1943, and was signed by Generalfeldmarschall Wilhelm Keitel. It was sent directly to Wisch's home address due to its large size. *Author's collection.*

Paul Hausser: Having joined the NSDAP on May 1, 1937, he was promoted to Gruppenführer in July 1939. Hausser led the SS/VT units within Panzerdivision "Kempf" during the Polish campaign in September 1939, earning the clasp to the Iron Cross second class. Effective October 19, 1939, Hausser commanded the SS-Verfügungsdivision (mot.), uniting regiments "Deutschland," "Germania," and "Der Führer." Promoted to Generalleutnant der Waffen-SS on November 19, 1939, he headed the Kommandoamt der Waffen-SS in addition to his divisional command from June to mid-August 1940. Hausser was awarded the clasp to the Iron Cross first class on May 17, 1940, and the Knight's Cross on August 8, 1941, during the campaign against Russia. He was promoted to Obergruppenführer on October 1, 1941, and was seriously wounded leading the then called Division "Reich." After his recovery, in late May 1942 Hausser formed and led SS-Generalkommando (later II.SS-Panzer-Korps) until June 28, 1944, when he became commander of the 7.Armee. He was awarded with the Oakleaves to the Knight's Cross on July 29, 1943. Promoted to Oberstgruppenführer on August 1, 1944, Hausser was severely wounded during the escape from the Falaise pocket on August 20, 1944. He was awarded the Swords to the Knight's Cross six days later. After his recovery in January 1945 Hausser was given command of Heeresgruppe "G" in the west, leading it until early April that year. He ended the war in Generalfeldmarschall Kesselnring's staff. Besides his previously mentioned awards for bravery and leadership, he was awarded the Golden Party Badge on January 30, 1943, and the Wound Badge in Silver on May 9, 1942. "Der Senior," or "Papa Hausser," as Paul Hausser was called by the men under his command, continued to be an active leader in the HIAG veterans' organization in post-war Germany until his death in Ludwigsburg on December 21, 1972, at the age of 92 (see footnote 28). *Photo courtesy of Mark C. Yerger.*

Theodor "Teddy" Wisch and Rudolf "Rudi" Sandig are seen here having a pleasant chat during May/June 1943. Sandig was one of the earliest members of the "Leibstandarte" and awarded the German Cross in Gold on January 25, 1942, as Hauptsturmführer and commander of the 7./LSSAH. He led the II./SS-Panzer-Grenadier Regiment 2 during the recapture of Kharkov and earned his Knight's Cross in the process on May 10, 1943. He later led SS-Panzer-Grenadier-Regiment 2 and ended the war as an Obersturmbannführer. Sandig died in Weyhe on August 11, 1994. *Author's collection.*

May 28, 1943: Sepp Dietrich proudly wears his Swords to the Knight's Cross and Gold Pilot Observer Badge with Diamonds on the occasion of his 51st birthday celebration, surrounded by men of his command. These include Sturmbannführer Bernhard Krause (top, second from left), then Flak Abteilung commander. He was awarded the Knight's Cross as commander of SS-Panzer-Grenadier-Regiment 26 on November 18, 1944, and was killed as an Obersturmbannführer in Muszla on February 19, 1945. Later Swords holder Kurt "Panzer" Meyer stands directly left of Dietrich. Later Oakleaves winner Hugo Kraas, standing right behind Dietrich, was then leading the I./SS-Panzer-Grenadier-Regiment 2. NCO Alfred Günther, wearing his open collar field gray assault gun uniform and Knight's Cross, won the award as an Oberscharführer on March 3, 1943, as a platoon leader of the 1./SS-Sturmgeschütz Abteilung. He was killed in action in Normandy on June 26, 1944. Albert Frey, to Dietrich's right wearing his Bronze Infantry Assault Badge, later commanded SS-Panzer-Grenadier Regiment 1. Hermann Weiser, far right, was Dietrich's adjutant and had won the Knight's Cross on April 1, 1943, leading the 2./Kradschützen Kompanie of the "Leibstandarte" reconnaissance detachment. He served as Korps Adjutant (IIa) of II.SS-Panzer Korps in 1944 and died on March 27, 1970, in Ludwigsburg. *Courtesy of Solkors-Collection.*

Sepp Dietrich and "Teddy" Wisch inspect the Panzer Werkstattkompanie as part of the divisional command exchange. To the left accompanying them is Hauptsturmführer Alfred Gilles, the later Divisional Engineer and commander of the "Leibstandarte" Instandsetzungsabteilung (maintenance detachment). Gilles (SS# 26 410) was born in Traben-Trabach on January 6, 1912. As an Obersturmführer he previously served with the 4./V./LSSAH in 1941 before moving the following year to become TFK of the Sturmgeschutzabteilung. By January 1943 Gilles moved to the Panzer Regiment as a Hauptsturmführer. He survived the war and died on February 23, 1986. Below: June 4, 1943: the command exchange of the "Leibstandarte" is complete. Standartenführer Wisch and Obergruppenführer Dietrich enjoy a glass of "Fernet Stock" herbal bitter. Standing in the background is Hauptsturmführer and Knight's Cross holder Hermann Weiser, the adjutant of the I.SS-Panzer Korps. *Author's collection.*

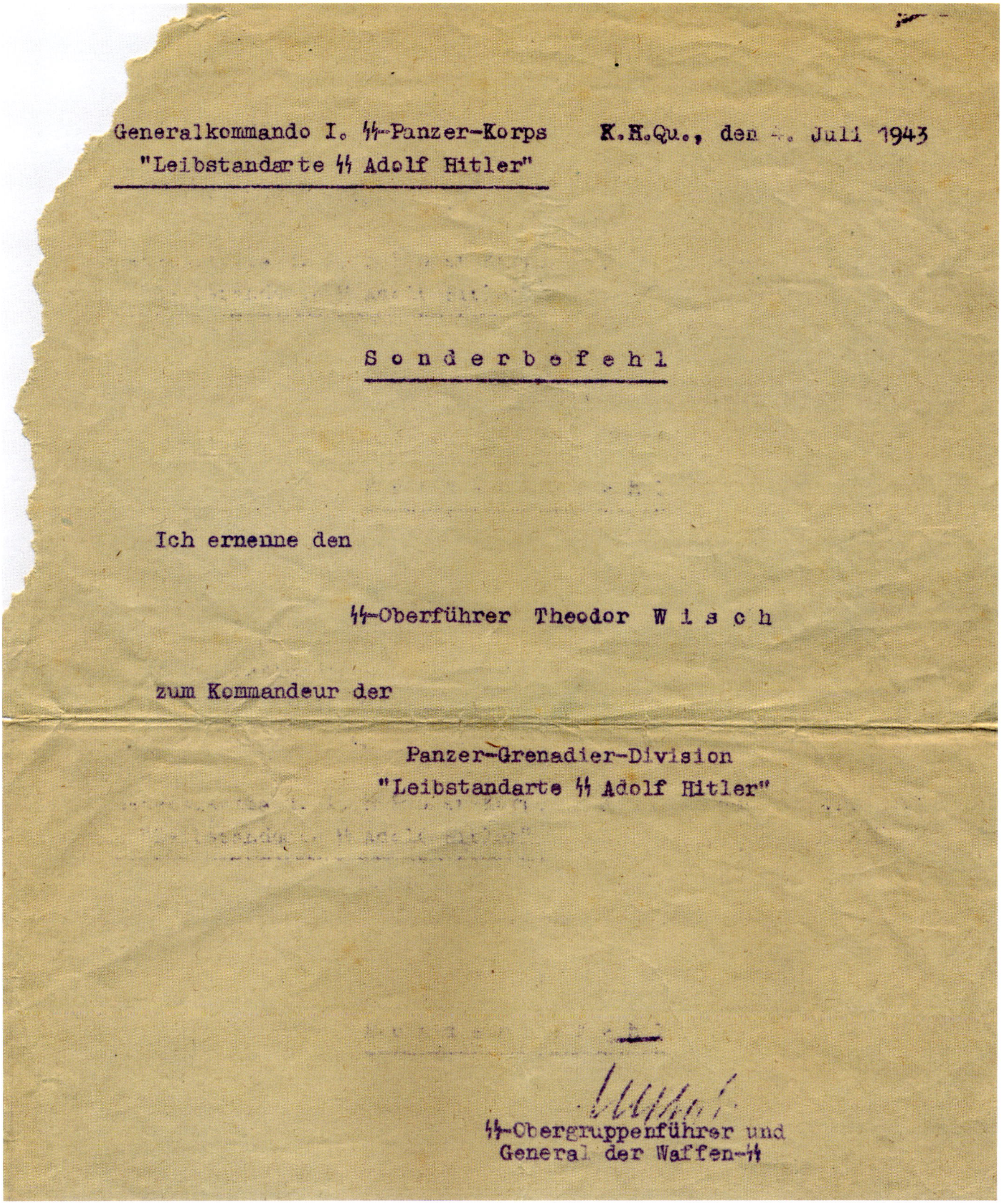

Generalkommando I. SS-Panzer-Korps K.H.Qu., den 4. Juli 1943
"Leibstandarte SS Adolf Hitler"

S o n d e r b e f e h l

Ich ernenne den

SS-Oberführer Theodor W i s c h

zum Kommandeur der

Panzer-Grenadier-Division
"Leibstandarte SS Adolf Hitler"

SS-Obergruppenführer und
General der Waffen-SS

The original "Sonderbefehl," dated July 4, 1943, appointing Oberführer Wisch to command the 1.SS-Panzer-Grenadier-Division "Leibstandarte." The order was issued by Generalkommando I.SS-Panzer-Korps "Leibstandarte" and is signed by Obergruppenführer Josef Dietrich. *Author's collection.*

Fritz Witt was born in Hohenlimburg on May 25, 1908. Completing school in 1925, he worked as a textile salesman until mid-1931. Joining the NSDAP and SS on December 1, 1931, Witt first served with the 1./II./30.SS-Standarte in Hagen. Transferred while a Truppführer to the SS-Sonderkommando "Berlin" on March 17, 1933, he became a Haupttruppführer on September 3, 1933. Commissioned on October 1, 1933, serving with the early "Leibstandarte," Witt was promoted to Obersturmführer on May 9, 1934. He moved to command the eventual 3./Deutschland on January 12, 1935, and there was promoted to Hauptsturmführer on June 1, 1935. Witt led the 3.Kompanie in Poland and won both classes of the Iron Cross (September 19 and 25, 1939). He then took command of the I./Deutschland on October 1, 1939, which he led during the Western campaign, resulting in an early award of the Knight's Cross on September 4, 1940. Leaving "Deutschland," Witt took command of the III./Leibstandarte on October 16, 1940, and from March 26, 1941, led the I.Bataillon. Promoted to Obersturmbannführer on November 27, 1941, he won the German Cross in Gold on February 8, 1942, before taking command of SS-Infanterie Regiment 1 on July 1, 1942. Promoted to Standartenführer on January 30, 1943, Witt also won the Oakleaves on March 1, 1943. An Oberführer since July 4, 1943, he became the first commander of the 12.SS-Panzer-Division "Hitlerjugend" on July 31, 1943. Among the youngest to achieve Brigadeführer and Generalmajor der Waffen-SS rank when promoted on April 20, 1944, Fritz Witt was killed by Allied naval fire at his divisional headquarters near Cean-Viseuc on June 14, 1944. *Photo courtesy of Mark C. Yerger.*

Sepp Dietrich: For combats leading the "Leibstandarte" in the Polish campaign Sepp Dietrich won clasps to his WWI Iron Crosses (25 and 27 September), and then the Knight's Cross on July 5, 1940, for the Western campaign. He became a General der Waffen-SS (added to his prior rank) on October 1, 1941, and won the Oakleaves to the Knight's Cross on December 31, 1941. The "Leibstandarte" expanded and was designated a Panzer-Grenadier-Division on September 9, 1942. Dietrich then won the Swords to the Knight's Cross on March 16, 1943, for the battles to retake Kharkov. He was succeeded in command of the "Leibstandarte" by Theodor Wisch on July 4, 1943. Dietrich then moved to command of the new I.SS-Panzerkorps on July 27, 1943. On August 1, 1944, he was uniquely promoted to Oberstgruppenführer und Panzer-Generaloberst der Waffen-SS. Dietrich next led the 5.Panzerarmee, and won the Diamonds to the Knight's Cross on August 6, 1944. His final command was the eventual 6.SS-Panzer-Armee from September 14, 1944, until the end of the war (see footnotes 6 and 39). *Courtesy of Hans-Peter Rackete.*

Above: Sepp Dietrich (left) and Wisch outside the Division's command post in December 1943. Note that Dietrich wears his platinum LAH ring, a gift from his men on the occasion of the fourth anniversary of the "Leibstandarte" on March 17, 1937. Below: Obergruppenführer Dietrich wears a tailored white sheepskin winter jacket while talking to First General Staff Officer (Ia) Rudolf Lehmann (back to the camera). On the left Oberführer Wisch wears a peaked visor cap. Dietrich is accompanied by his adjutant, Hauptsturmführer and Knight's Cross holder Hermann Weiser, who stands at right wearing an enlisted man's coat. *Author's collection.*

November 15, 1943, in Zydouce, Russia: Oberführer Wisch with his First Staff Officer (Ia) Sturmbannführer Rudolf "Rudi" Lehmann (right) and Lehmann's orderly (O1) Hauptsturmführer Ralf Tiemann (left). Tiemann won the German Cross in Gold on December 2, 1943, leading the 7./Panzer-Regiment 1. He ended the war as a Sturmbannführer and also served as "Leibstandarte" Ia. In the postwar years Tiemann wrote a history of the 7.Kompanie and completed the official history of the "Leibstandarte" after the death of Lehmann. Ralf Tiemann died on May 19, 2005. *Author's collection.* Kotowka, December 13, 1943: after paying the division's command post a brief visit to congratulate Oberführer Wisch on his birthday, General der Panzertruppe Erhard Raus drives off in his command car. To the rear of the car wearing his German Cross in Gold is Sturmbannführer Rudolf Lehmann, the divisional Ia. *Author's collection.*

Rudolf Lehmann was born in Heidelberg on January 30, 1914, entering the SS on March 8, 1933, and becoming an SS-Mann on 8 May that year. Lehmann joined the "Leibstandarte" on May 11, 1933, being promoted to Sturmmann on 1 August, and to Unterscharführer on April 1, 1934. He attended the 1935 class at Junkerschule Bad Tölz and was commissioned on April 20, 1936. Assigned to Regiment "Germania," Lehmann undertook a platoon leader course before leading similar size units within the Regiment. Promoted to Obersturmführer on September 1, 1938, he led the armored car platoon of "Germania" during the Polish campaign and won the Iron Cross Second Class on November 15, 1939. Taking command of the 14./Germania in April 1940, he was promoted to Hauptsturmführer on July 1, 1940. Leading his Kompanie successfully during the Western Campaign, he was awarded the Iron Cross First Class on May 29, 1940. Lehmann returned to the "Leibstandarte" in October 1940, serving as the Brigade ordnance officer (01) until April 1, 1941. Severely wounded in August 1941, he had been acting "Leibstandarte" First General Staff Officer (Ia). After his recovery Lehmann attended a General Staff course with the Army from March to May 1942. He next resumed the post of Ia on July 1, 1942, serving under Sepp Dietrich and Theodor Wisch until May 25, 1944. Promoted to Sturmbannführer on September 1, 1942, Lehmann won the German Cross in Gold on November 1, 1943, and the Knight's Cross on February 23, 1944, both being recommended by Theodor Wisch. Promoted to Obersturmbannführer on January 30, 1944, Lehmann was Chief of Staff of the I.SS-Panzer-Korps from October 1, 1944, to March 9, 1945. Promoted to Standartenführer on January 30, 1945, he was given command of the 2.SS-Panzer-Division "Das Reich" on March 10, 1945. On May 6, 1945, Lehmann was awarded the Oakleaves to the Knight's Cross for leadership of that division during the retreat in Austria. Rudolf "Rudi" Lehmann wrote the first three volumes of the "Leibstandarte" divisional history before he passed away on September 17, 1983, in Ettlingen. *Courtesy of Mark C. Yerger.*

Wisch is seen on top of his command vehicle observing the outcome of a spring 1944 attack near Shitomir. *Author's collection*. Below: Sepp Dietrich visiting the "Leibstandarte" Reconnaissance Detachment near Kharkov. In the background (left) is later Oberscharführer Jupp Steinbüchel, Dietrich and Wisch's radio operator. *Courtesy of Mike Smeets*.

January 30, 1944: Wisch and Panzer Regiment commander Joachim Peiper congratulate Michael Wittmann on his award of the Knight's Cross with Oakleaves. He was also promoted to Obersturmführer d.R. The very same day Wisch was promoted to Brigadeführer. At that time Wittmann and his crew had destroyed 117 enemy tanks. *Author's collection.*

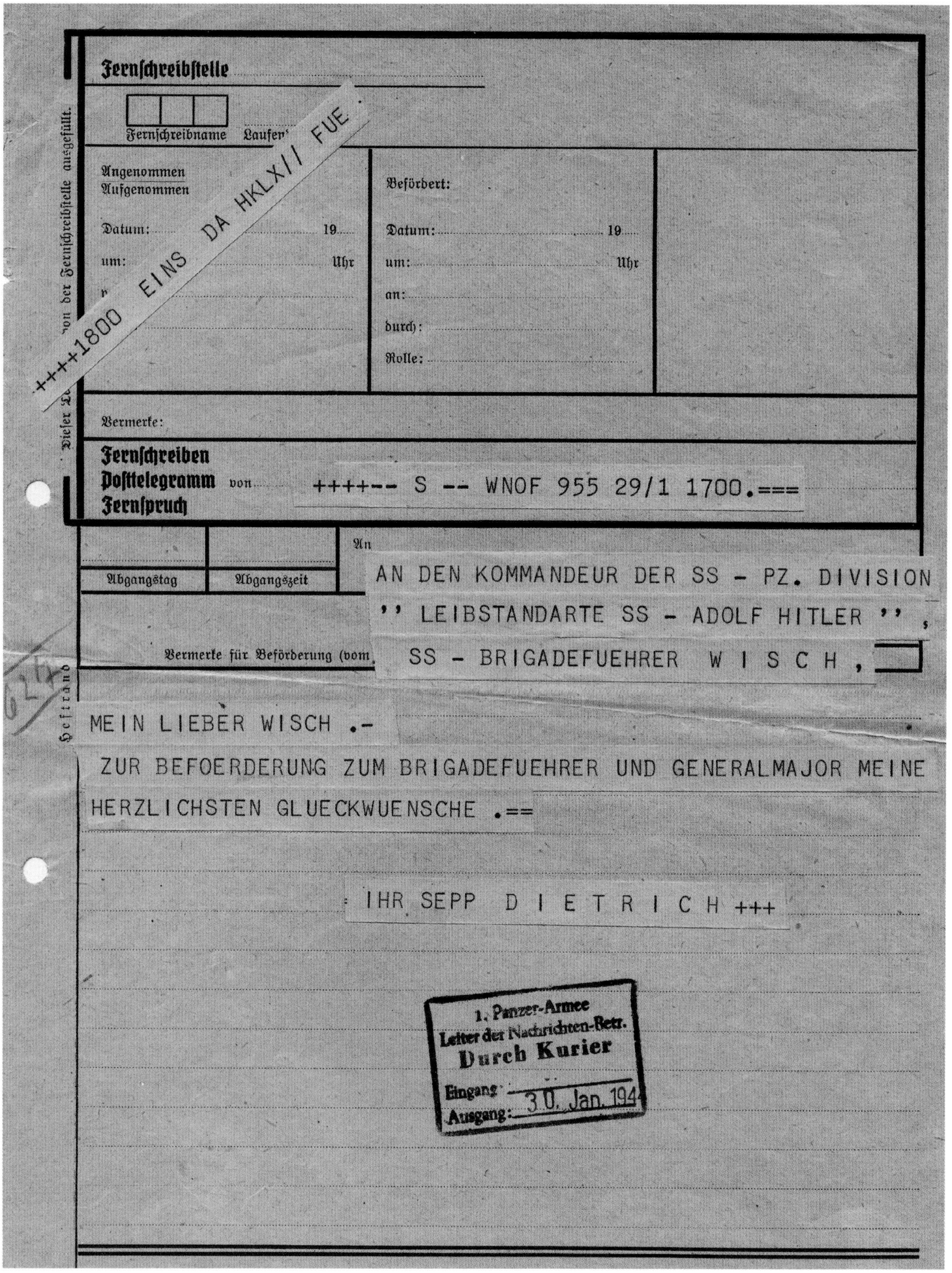

Fernschreibstelle

Fernschreibname Laufer

Angenommen / Aufgenommen

Datum: 19

um: Uhr

Befördert:

Datum: 19

um: Uhr

an:

durch:

Rolle:

++++1800 EINS DA HKLXII FUE .

Vermerke:

Fernschreiben / Posttelegramm / Fernspruch von ++++-- S -- WNOF 955 29/1 1700.===

Abgangstag | Abgangszeit

An

AN DEN KOMMANDEUR DER SS - PZ. DIVISION
" LEIBSTANDARTE SS - ADOLF HITLER " ,
SS - BRIGADEFUEHRER W I S C H ,

Vermerke für Beförderung (vom

MEIN LIEBER WISCH .-
ZUR BEFOERDERUNG ZUM BRIGADEFUEHRER UND GENERALMAJOR MEINE HERZLICHSTEN GLUECKWUENSCHE .==

IHR SEPP D I E T R I C H +++

1. Panzer-Armee
Leiter der Nachrichten-Betr.
Durch Kurier
Eingang:
Ausgang: 30. Jan. 1944

A telegram sent by Sepp Dietrich to Wisch dated January 30, 1944, reads: "My dear Wisch – For the promotion to Brigadeführer and Generalmajor my sincere congratulations. Yours, Sepp Dietrich." Note that Dietrich addresses Wisch with "Ihr" in formal German language. It is a myth that communication, written or verbal, with Dietrich was usually on an informal basis. *Author's collection.*

Above: Hitler and Wisch shake hands before the latter is bestowed the Oakleaves at the Berghof on March 13, 1944. (Courtesy Mark C. Yerger) Below: Invited officers of the "Leibstandarte" and "Hitlerjugend," including Fritz Witt, Max Wünsche, Sepp Dietrich, and Wisch, have a casual conversation with Hitler after the ceremony. *Author's collection.*

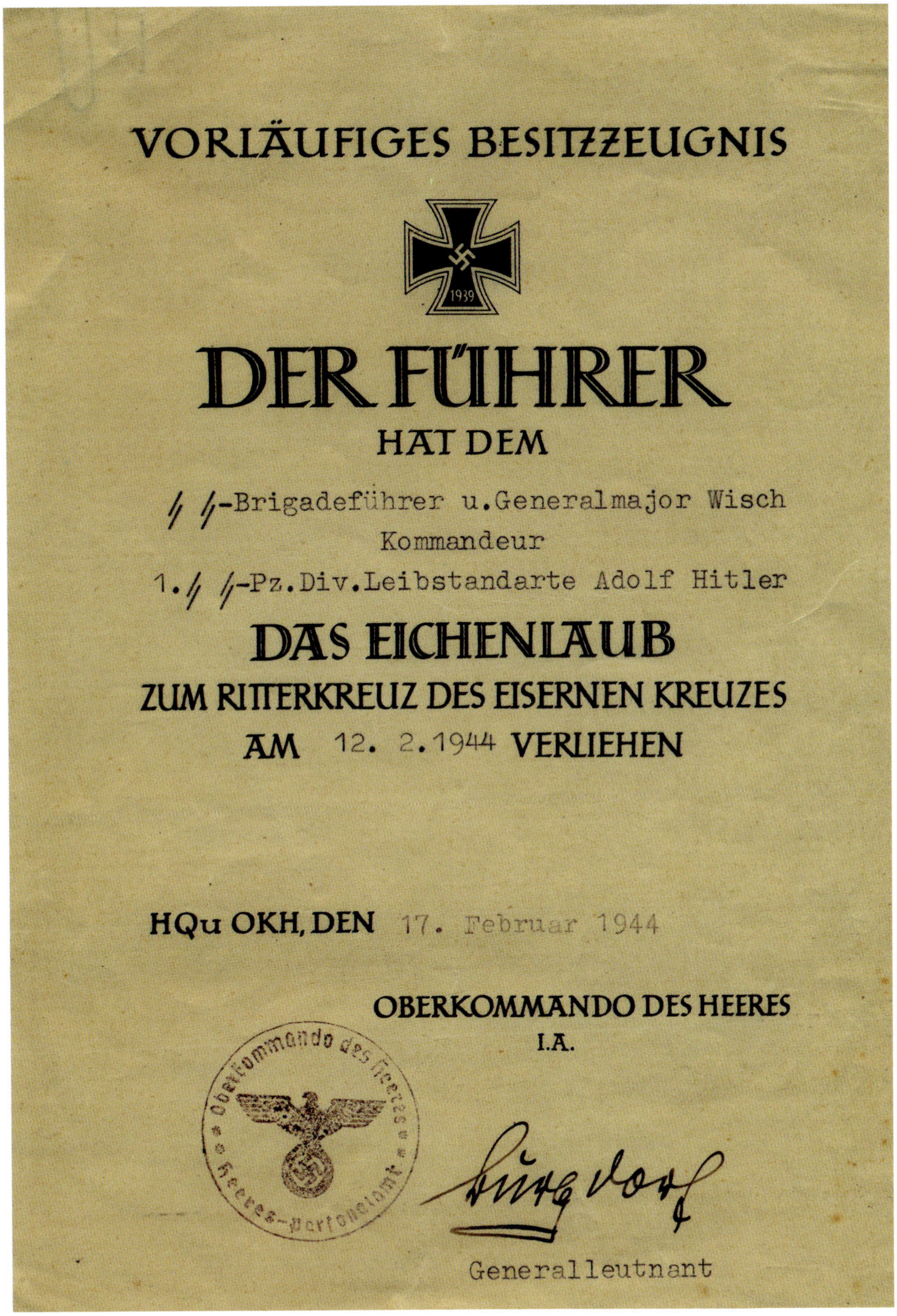

VORLÄUFIGES BESITZZEUGNIS

DER FÜHRER

HAT DEM

SS-Brigadeführer u.Generalmajor Wisch

Kommandeur

1.SS-Pz.Div.Leibstandarte Adolf Hitler

DAS EICHENLAUB

ZUM RITTERKREUZ DES EISERNEN KREUZES

AM 12. 2.1944 VERLIEHEN

HQu OKH, DEN 17. Februar 1944

OBERKOMMANDO DES HEERES

I.A.

Oberkommando des Heeres · Heeres-Personalamt ·

Burgdorf

Generalleutnant

Wisch's preliminary award document for the Oakleaves was signed by Generalleutnant Wilhelm Burgdorf. Note the effort the office clerk undertook to produce runic SS letters for this document with a standard typewriter. Normal lettering was generally used on these types of documents when issued by the Heeres-Personalamt (Army Administration Office). *Author's collection.*

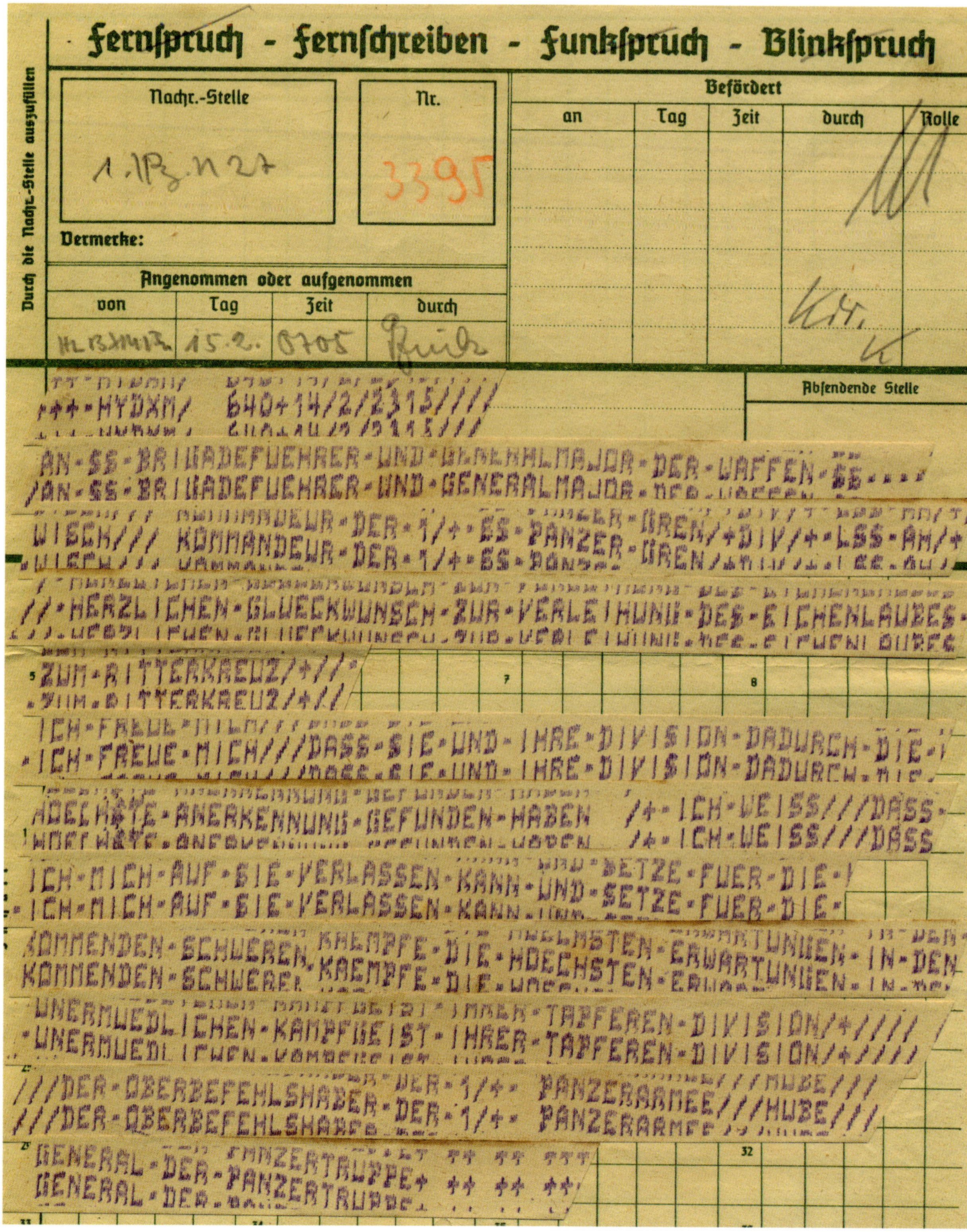

Fernspruch - Fernschreiben - Funkspruch - Blinkspruch

Durch die Nachr.-Stelle auszufüllen

Nachr.-Stelle: 1.Pz.N 27 | Nr.: 3395

Vermerke:

Angenommen oder aufgenommen — von: H.L.B.H.M.I.Z. | Tag: 15.2. | Zeit: 0705 | durch: [illegible]

Befördert — an | Tag | Zeit | durch | Rolle

Absendende Stelle

+++-HYDXM/ 640+14/2/2315////

AN-SS-BRIGADEFUEHRER-UND-GENERALMAJOR-DER-WAFFEN-SS....

WISCH/// KOMMANDEUR-DER-1/+-SS-PANZER-GREN/+DIV/+-LSS-AH/+

//-HERZLICHEN-GLUECKWUNSCH-ZUR-VERLEIHUNG-DES-EICHENLAUBES-

ZUM-RITTERKREUZ/+//

ICH-FREUE-MICH///DASS-SIE-UND-IHRE-DIVISION-DADURCH-DIE-

HOECHSTE-ANERKENNUNG-GEFUNDEN-HABEN /+-ICH-WEISS///DASS

ICH-MICH-AUF-SIE-VERLASSEN-KANN-UND-SETZE-FUER-DIE-

KOMMENDEN-SCHWEREN-KAEMPFE-DIE-HOECHSTEN-ERWARTUNGEN-IN-DEN-

UNERMUEDLICHEN-KAMPFGEIST-IHRER-TAPFEREN-DIVISION/+////

///DER-OBERBEFEHLSHABER-DER-1/+- PANZERARMEE///HUBE///

GENERAL-DER-PANZERTRUPPE+ ++ ++ ++

Diamonds winner Hans Hube congratulates Wisch on his Oakleaves to the Knight's Cross with this telex: "Congratulations on the Oakleaves to the Knight's Cross. I am happy that you and your Division through this have attained high recognition. I know that I can rely on you to put my highest expectations in the never-ending combat spirit of your brave division in the heavy battles to come. The Supreme Commander of the 1.Panzer Armee, Hube, General der Panzertruppe." Ironically, ten years earlier Hube, at the time commander of the Army's Infanterie Schule Döberitz, had evaluated Wisch as insufficiently skilled and incapable of being an infantry platoon leader! *Author's collection.*

After Wisch received the Oakleaves from Adolf Hitler are (from left) Hauptsturmführer Otto Günsche, Oberführer Fritz Witt, Obergruppenführer Sepp Dietrich, Wisch, and Obersturmbannführer Max Wünsche. Hitler´s photographer, Heinrich Hoffmann, took the image in one of the private rooms at the Berghof. Note that both Dietrich and Wünsche wear their black tank uniforms. Below: accompanied by his wife (left), Wisch takes a walk near Hitler's Berghof after having received his Oakleaves to the Knight's Cross. *Author's collection.*

Theodor Wisch relaxing shortly before the 1944 Normandy invasion. *Private collection.* Below: March 6, 1944, Heinrich Himmler and Brigadeführer Wisch visit the Versuchsgut Pabenschwandt/Plainfeld, 10 kilometers east of Salzburg, Austria. *Author's collection.*

Wisch (left) awards the Knight's Cross to Sturmbannführer Gustav Knittel (Reconnaissance Detachment commander) and Hauptsturmführer Paul Guhl (III./SS-Panzer-Grenadier Regiment 2 commander) in mid-June 1944. Both received their awards for combats during the southern Ukraine campaign of early 1944. Below left: in the weeks before the Normandy invasion entertainment was staged for the officers, NCOs, and troops. Here Wisch observes a fellow comrade and German Cross holder receiving ammunition during a pistol competition. Below right: the famous portrait photo of Brigadeführer Theodor Wisch, taken in May 1944. *Author's collection.*

Wilhelm Mohnke was born in Lübeck on March 15, 1911. He became an SS-Mann on November 16, 1931, serving in the 4.SS-Standarte of his hometown until January 1932, when he was transferred to the I./22.SS-Standarte. Promoted to Truppführer on March 9, 1933, Mohnke was among the original 117 men of the SS-Sonderkommando led by Josef Dietrich. Serving with guard details at the Reich Chancellery and other government facilities, Mohnke attended a platoon leader course at the Army's Infantry Training school in Döberitz. On July 18, 1933, he was given command of the 2.Sturm, being commissioned a Sturmführer on 28 June then promoted to Sturmhauptführer on October 1, 1933. On October 17, 1934, the Standarte was reorganized and Mohnke took command of the 5./LAH, leading it until May 28, 1940. He won both Classes of the Iron Cross (1 September and 8 November) in the 1939 Polish campaign. Mohnke then led the II.Bataillon, being promoted to Sturmbannführer on September 1, 1940. Leading Kampfgruppe "Mohnke" in Yugoslavia, he was severely wounded in the leg during a bombing raid on April 6, 1941, being evacuated to Berlin for extensive medical treatment. On December 26, 1941, Mohnke won one of the earliest German Crosses in Gold. After recovering, he promoted the creation of a tank unit for the "Leibstandarte," but never led its armored detachment, instead being transferred to command the "Leibstandarte" replacement battalion. Promoted to Obersturmbannführer on June 21, 1943, Mohnke next commanded SS-Panzer-Grenadier-Regiment 26 of the 12.SS-Panzer-Division "Hitlerjugend." There he was promoted to Standartenführer on June 21, 1944, and won the Knight's Cross on July 21, 1944. After Theodor Wisch was wounded on August 20, 1944, Mohnke took command of the "Leibstandarte." Promoted to Oberführer on November 4, 1944, he led the Division during the Ardennes Offensive and became a Brigadeführer on January 30, 1945. Succeeded by Otto Kumm as "Leibstandarte" commander on February 6, 1945, he was ordered to Berlin. There Mohnke commanded 2,000 volunteers of the "Leibstandarte" Wachbattalion, Ersatzabteilung, and the divisional remnants of "Charlemangne" defending the Reichs Chancellery. After Hitler's suicide, Mohnke was captured leading a breakout attempt from the capital and was held in solitary confinement by Russia until 1949. Finally released from the Woikowo Generals prison on October 10, 1955, Wilhelm "Willy" Mohnke died on August 6, 2001, in Rahlstedt, near Hamburg. *Courtesy of Mark C. Yerger.*

Brigadeführer Theodor Wisch wearing his Oakleaves to the Knight's Cross in a May 1944 photo shortly before D-Day. Years later Wisch inscribed this original wartime photo "With kind regards Theodor Wisch" as a present to his half-brother, Waldemar Heinrich. *Author's collection.*

Hans Bernhard was born on December 22, 1919, in Nonnenweier and joined the SS on November 1, 1938 (SS# 367 333). He served with the 12.(schw. MG)/Deutschland and saw combat in the 1939 Polish Campaign. From February 1 to May 5, 1940, Bernhard was in the first wartime reserve officers' class at Junkerschule Braunschweig. Volunteering for the artillery, he also attended an officer training course at the Army's Artillerie Schule in Jüterbog from May 20 to August 9, 1940, being commissioned an Untersturmführer d.R. on August 1, 1940. Bernhard was regimental ordnance officer of the "Leibstandarte" Artillerie Regiment, later transferring to the 5./Artillerie-Regiment as a forward observer in the Greek campaign, where he won the Iron Cross 2nd Class. He held the same post in the Russian campaign, wining the Iron Cross 1st Class at Rollbahn Nord in July 1941 from a personal recommendation by Fritz Witt, with Sepp Dietrich approving the award. Promoted to Obersturmführer d.R. on April 20, 1942, in the 1943 recapture of Kharkov, he served as adjutant of the II./Artillerie Regiment and commanded the 8.Batterie during the battle for Kursk, until being wounded on July 13, 1943. In February 1944 Bernhard took an Artillerie Abteilung commander training course and was promoted to Hauptsturmführer d.R. on April 20, 1944. He then served as staff Ic of the "Leibstandarte" from July 1, 1944, before being acting Ia after Erich Grensing was severely wounded. Bernhard then served as the staff O1 in Hungary and Austria. He also acted as functional leader of the "Leibstandarte" Artillerie Regiment after division commander Kumm lost faith in Obersturmbannführer Steineck's abilities. Both a friend and extraordinary help to the author, Hans Bernhard died on October 2, 2010. *Author's collection.*

Otto Kumm was born in Hamburg on October 1, 1909, and joined the SS in his home town on December 1, 1931, with the 1./I./28.SS-Standarte in his birth town. After taking command of the III.Sturmbann in March 1934, he transferred to the Political Readiness Detachment in Hamburg that formally became Regiment "Germania" in September 1936. Kumm led the 4.(MG)/Germania from May 17, 1935, to December 10, 1936, before being transferred to the 2./Deutschland in February 1937. Promoted to Hauptsturmführer on September 13, 1936, he moved to the new SS-Standarte 3 "Der Führer" that was formed on May 1, 1938, as 10.Kompanie Chef. During the 1940 Western Campaign, he earned both classes of the Iron Cross (29 May and 4 June) and the Wound Badge in Black on June 8, 1940. Promoted to Sturmbannführer on September 1, 1940, Kumm was given command of "Der Führer" on July 11, 1941. He won the German Cross in Gold as an Obersturmbannführer on December 3, 1941, and the Knight's Cross on February 16, 1942, for combats near Rshew. Kumm continued in command at Kharkov and won the Oakleaves, the first for "Das Reich," on April 6, 1943. Promoted to Standartenführer on April 20, 1943, he became the Chief of Staff of the V.SS-Gebirgs-Korps on May 1, 1943, and was promoted to Oberführer on January 30, 1944. Kumm then took command of the 7.SS-Gebrigs-Division "Prinz Eugen" in February 1944. Promoted to Brigadeführer on November 9, 1944, he succeeded Wilhelm Mohnke as the final commander of the "Leibstandarte." The Division was only a shadow of what it once was, as related to the author at Kumm's home in Offenburg. Recommended for the Swords while serving with "Prinz Eugen," Otto Kumm won the award on March 17, 1945, before leading the "Leibstandarte" into U.S. captivity on May 8, 1945. Living in Hamburg after the war, he was the founder of HIAG, the Reciprocal Aid Society of Former Members of the Waffen-SS. Kumm was awarded the HIAG Diamonds award for 50 years of contribution during HIAG-Hamburg's 50th anniversary meeting in 2000. Otto Kumm died on March 23, 2004. *Courtesy of Mark C. Yerger.*

Wisch in 1992 with his friend "Das Reich" Knight's Cross holder Ernst Barkmann. *Author's collection.* Below: Group photo taken on Heinz Macher's birthday with fellow Knight's Cross holders. From left are Heinrich Springer, Ernst Barkmann, Macher, Eichler (Army), Theodor Wisch, Günther Wisliceny, Albert Stenwedel, Willi Hein and Werner Meyer. *Courtesy of Patrick Ott.*